Assault Crossing

Assault Crossing

The River Seine 1944

Roger M. Clemons
P. O. Box 102
Bartlett, NH 03812

Ken Ford

Pen & Sword
MILITARY

First published in Great Britain in 1988 by
David & Charles Publishers

This edition published in 2011 by
Pen & Sword Military
an imprint of
Pen & Sword Books Ltd
47 Church Street
Barnsley
South Yorkshire
S70 2AS

ISBN 978-1-84884-576-3

Typeset in 11pt Ehrhardt by
Mac Style, Beverley, East Yorkshire

Printed and bound in the UK by
CPI

Pen & Sword Books Ltd incorporates the Imprints of Pen & Sword Aviation,
Pen & Sword Family History, Pen & Sword Maritime, Pen & Sword Military,
Pen & Sword Discovery, Wharncliffe Local History, Wharncliffe True Crime,
Wharncliffe Transport, Pen & Sword Select, Pen & Sword Military Classics,
Leo Cooper, The Praetorian Press, Remember When, Seaforth Publishing and
Frontline Publishing.

For a complete list of Pen & Sword titles please contact
PEN & SWORD BOOKS LIMITED
47 Church Street, Barnsley, South Yorkshire, S70 2AS, England
E-mail: enquiries@pen-and-sword.co.uk
Website: www.pen-and-sword.co.uk

Contents

To the four ladies in my life
Valda, Amanda, Joanne and Katelyn

Author's Original Acknowledgements

I would like to extend my sincere thanks to all who have helped me in the preparation of this book. By far the most satisfying aspect of my research was the opportunity to meet so many helpful people. My faith in human nature has been constantly reinforced by their kindness and enthusiasm.

First, I must thank Algy Grubb, who remains the inspiration for this book. A chance meeting with him on a trip to the Normandy beaches led to our having a long chat about his experiences at Vernon. It was from this that I developed a strong desire to know more about those events on the River Seine over forty years ago. I shall be eternally grateful for his help, encouragement and advice, without which this book could never have been written.

I would also like to acknowledge the invaluable help of others and pay special thanks to the following who were able to give information about the battle:

43rd Division
Major J.F. Milne, Colonel D.I.M. Robbins, V. Coombs, N. Smith, K. Borroughs, H. Brown, L. Wrintmore, R.C. Bolton, A.E. Hazell, G.R. Butcher, A. Kings, K.J. Lugg, D. Hodgkins, J. Haynes, E.W. Tipping, K.M. White, Colonel M.P. Concannon, W.S. Drew, R. Barker, Major-General H.A. Borradaile, W.J. Chalmers, Brigadier G. Taylor, F. Grigg, J. Foster, Major D. Durie, H.G.W. Drake, A.P.A. Tucker, R. Hunt, B. Offer, F. Greenwood, A.R. Hitchcock, Major J.M.F. Hutchinson, J. Meredith, G. Salisbury, Lieutenant-Colonel R.S. Williams-Thomas, P. Spencer Moore, K. Williams, S. Beard, J.A. Bartlett.

4th/7th Dragoon Guards
R. Cox, Major-General Sir James d'Avidgor Goldsmid, Major M.A. Trasenster.

49th Field Surgical Unit
Dr G. L. Haines.

In France
Maurice Levoin, Gabriel Valet, Louis and Ezra Le Maignan, Guy Dugrés, RenéVan Florop, George Azémia, Louise Damasse, Jacques Cambuza, Louis and Jermaine Neuvilly.

I wish to thank the Imperial War Museum, the War Office Library, the National Archives at Kew, the Dorset Military Museum, the Department of Geography University of Keele, the Royal Artillery Institute, the Somerset Light Infantry Regimental Museum, the Royal Engineers Museum, and the Tank Museum Bovington for their assistance during my research.

I also owe a debt of gratitude to all those people who helped me assemble, translate and produce the wealth of details that went into this book: Adam Sisman, Sue Dean, Susie Penrose, Bob and Gilberte Cozens, Pat and Trevor Lucas and Kate Durham.

I would like to acknowledge all the kind assistance and hospitality that I received on my visits to Vernon: Monique Artero and her staff at the Bibliothèque Municipale deVernon, Alexandra Delaunay, Claire and Phillipe Brossel, Liliane Charles, Jean Castreau and Françoise Paris. I should also like to thank the Mayor of Vernon, Jean-Claude Asphé, for the facilities that he placed at my disposal.

I am also grateful for permission to use quotations from the following: *The 43rd Wessex Division at War: 1944–1945* by H. Essame; *Corps Commander* by Sir Brian Horrocks; *The Seine! The Seine!* by T. Lloyd; *The Maroon Square* by Majors A.D. Parsons, D.I.M. Robbins and D.C. Gilson; 'The Royal Engineers Journal Vol LXIV No 1'; and *The 4th Somerset Light Infantry Regimental History* by C.G. Lipscombe.

In closing, I offer a very special thanks for the patience and understanding of my wife Valda and my daughters Amanda and Joanne during the preparation of this book.

Ken Ford
September 1987

Preface to the New Edition

It is now almost twenty-five years since *Assault Crossing* was first published, and in that time many things have changed. When I wrote this, my first book, the battle was virtually unknown. It was seen as just a small action in which one British division was pitted against a single German formation. In the grand scheme of things, it was no more than a minor skirmish. Now many memorials have sprouted up around the sites associated with the action and this assault crossing of the River Seine has achieved a historical identity of its own. The Royal Engineers have used the battle to train future soldiers, university students have written dissertations on it and the French people have discovered their own role in the battle. This type of book can now no longer be written, for those who participated in the Second World War are rapidly fading away. I commend my publishers Pen & Sword for producing this reprint and allowing a new generation to read the story of those men of 43rd (Wessex) Division who fought so courageously at Vernon in August 1944.

Ken Ford
April 2011

Introduction

The River Seine, flowing as it does south-east to north-west, forms a natural barrier to the passage of armies across northern France. Once the Allied planners had decided on Normandy as the site of the invasion, the great river presented two opposing facets to any formulation of strategy. First, it became an aid to defence during the build-up of strength after the landings and, second, it formed an obstacle to expansion when the fighting had moved on out of Normandy towards Germany.

Prior to the opening of this 'second front' in the war in Europe, all the bridges across the Seine between Paris and the sea were destroyed, as were those across the River Loire, so as to help seal off the lodgement area and complicate any German attempts to reinforce the region. For the first few months after the invasion, the Allies saw the wide unbridged Seine as a useful defensive moat helping to keep Normandy isolated from the rest of France. Its usefulness would continue later, if and when they finally won the battle for control of Normandy and began to gain ground, for the retreating Germans would find themselves again hampered by the wide waterway as they were forced further and further eastwards.

Once the German army had been pushed back across the river things would change. At that point the Seine would become a problem for the Allies, for the river would by then cease to be of strategic use and instead become a formidable barrier to their expansion of the bridgehead.

The original invasion plan, operation 'Overlord', estimated that the River Seine would be reached at around D-Day plus ninety days (4 September 1944). It was feared that the German army would have a defensive line prepared on the river by that time and so the Allied Expeditionary Forces would be forced to halt there to allow the troops to rest, replenish their equipment, receive reinforcements and prepare for the next part of the great trek across northern France towards Germany.

The Allied invasion of France by British, Canadian and American forces took place in Normandy on 6 June 1944, along a fifty-mile front stretching from the mouth of the River Orne in the east to the base of the Cotentin Peninsula in the west. Once ashore, the battle for the bridgehead began. The fighting that took place over the next few months proved to be the most vicious and costly during the campaign in north-western Europe.

For the whole of June, July and most of August, a determined enemy kept the Allied armies bottled up in the confines of Normandy. Week by week, more and more troops poured ashore and into the battle. The enemy pitted its best formations against the invaders. The result was a war of attrition; casualties on both sides were horrendous. It was a battle in which, as time went by, the tide inexorably turned in favour of the Allies, for the sheer weight of numbers of men and machines arriving over the open beaches more than matched those brought forward by the enemy, over damaged road and rail systems that were continually attacked by British and American aircraft.

Even as early as 17 June, it appeared to some of the German commanders that Normandy would have to be abandoned to the Allies. By that time, they had come to realise that the British and American armies could no longer be thrown back into the sea as had been first envisaged.

At a meeting in Soissons between Hitler and his commanders in France, both Field Marshal Rommel (Commander German Army Group 'B') and Field Marshal Von Rundstedt (Commander-in-Chief West) urged Hitler to agree to a staged withdrawal to a new line based on the Seine, behind which the armoured divisions could be used more effectively. Hitler was furious. There would be no retreat; Normandy was to be defended at all costs. This was a decision that ultimately benefited the Allies most of all, for it committed the Germans to contest every foot of territory. Unable to withdraw to a more favourable position, they fought where they stood, a policy that eventually led to their defeat in Normandy.

By the middle of August, the remnants of the two German armies fighting in Normandy (Seventh Army and the Fifth Panzer Army) had been forced into a small pocket between Falaise and Argentan. Their withdrawal to the east quickly became a rout, as the survivors tried to escape before they were completely surrounded. Between the two towns the desperate enemy troops fought tenaciously to get as many men and machines as possible out of the trap. It was a killing ground, hemmed in on all sides and subjected to continual air attacks throughout the long hours of daylight; the casualties were appalling. Piles of charred wreckage, vehicles intertwined with men and animals, lay twisted in pathetic heaps. Lorries, cars, tanks and guns, halted by vast traffic jams that choked every lane and road, were smashed by rocket-firing Typhoon aircraft. As the Allies closed in, the area was subjected to further torture when massed artillery concentrations pounded the trapped enemy. This climax of the battle of Normandy should have ended in the complete destruction of both enemy armies, but some troops miraculously escaped eastwards to fight another day.

The ring was finally sealed on 20 August, but not without recriminations in the Allied camp. The final closing of the pocket was held up by misunderstandings between the British and Americans, which led to criticism of General Montgomery's handling of the affair, and many Germans slipped through the noose to head pell-mell for the Seine. Nevertheless, it was a considerable victory for the Allies. Hitler had suffered his biggest defeat since Stalingrad. Over 50,000 Germans had surrendered, between 10,000 and 20,000 men had been killed and almost all their tanks and heavy equipment had been lost. The battle for Normandy was over; in total the enemy had lost over 300,000 men killed, wounded or missing.

With this final collapse of the German forces in Normandy, the Americans were able to step up their mobile operations and began to fan out across north-western France. The sudden disintegration of enemy resistance also prompted a rethink of the tactics to be adopted for the next phase of the war. On 17 August, the Allied Supreme Commander, General Eisenhower, decided that the Allies would try to 'bounce' the Seine. He reasoned that the German army could never extricate itself from the Falaise débâcle and organise a defence on the river, as long as the Allies kept up the intense pressure all along the front line. Eisenhower therefore planned to cross the river in strength once it had been reached and then to push on and destroy the enemy between there and the River Somme.

This might seem an obvious decision to make (the relentless pursuit of a defeated enemy), but it did pose immense problems from a logistics point of view. At that time, only one port, Cherbourg, was available to the Allies. The majority of supplies were still being landed over open beaches in the bay of the Seine. During the fairly static fighting in Normandy, with the short supply lines between the coastline and the front, the daily discharge of men and *matériel* easily kept pace with consumption, but after the American breakout and the introduction of a more mobile type of warfare the demand for supplies began to reach crisis point. Events were unfolding with such speed that advance depots could no longer be established. The motorised divisions were consuming everything that could be sped forward to them. Nothing was left to stockpile; the supply lines led straight to the front line. Each new mile that was gained by the swift American thrusts placed a further strain on the motor transport bringing the supplies forward.

With a clear signal from their Supreme Commander to strike eastwards with all speed, the four Allied armies operating in Normandy (two American, one British and one Canadian) now set their sights on the Seine and beyond. This is the story of just one of the many crossings of the River Seine that took place in August 1944. It is an account of how one British division, set free from the closely knit Normandy countryside, raced over a hundred miles to the river and attacked the enemy–held far shore in broad daylight. It was an action which spanned just seven days from its inception to its completion. A tidy battle, self–contained almost, with one British division pitted against one German division. It was also an action that went down in military history as an 'epic operation' – an action that was to be used as an example in the training of future soldiers. However, in reality, the battle proceeded in perfect chaos, lumbering from crisis to crisis, its outcome depending partly on luck and partly on judgement. But, when all things are considered, is that not the way of war?

Prologue

The evening of 25 August 1944 was warm and sunny. For Major James Fraser Milne of the 5th Battalion Wiltshire Regiment, the day had been long, hot and dusty. Events had started well enough twelve hours earlier when he awoke in a peaceful Normandy pasture scores of miles from the nearest German soldier. With no evidence of any fighting to be seen, there was even the luxury of a leisurely cooked breakfast. However, by the time a quarter to seven that evening had arrived, Milne knew only too well that he was again back at the sharp end. He had been transported over forty miles (64km) to a town called Vernon and was poised to lead his men into action once more. Although he did not realise it at the time, his company had become the spearhead for the whole of the British army. The front line in the battle for Europe was just a few short yards away. Half-crouched behind a stone wall, and with the knowledge that the enemy overlooked him, he peered cautiously over the top.

Milne looked out across two grassy meadows towards the slopes of a steep chalk bluff that dominated the horizon. At the base of this spur were a few houses dotted alongside a road. As he scanned the road, his eyes settled for a moment on his company's objective, a large white house beneath the cliffs. Milne had been ordered to capture and hold the house to prevent any of the enemy moving down the valley. The house was just four hundred and fifty yards (411m) away across open terrain. But it was not just distance that separated the company commander from his objective, for between the two grassy meadows lay one of the great rivers of France: the Seine.

Major Milne's company, 'A' Company, had been chosen to lead the right-hand side of a two-pronged attack across the river. The two hundred yards (182m) of exposed water in front of Milne held no great fear for him. After all the horrors he and his men had endured during the earlier battles in Normandy, he faced his future with equanimity. It was after all just one more attack, albeit in the unusual role of water-borne infantry. The crossing itself would only take a few minutes and once the troops had arrived on dry land it would be business as usual. What concerned him most of all was the efficiency of the smoke-screen that was to cover the assault. Was it, he thought, possible for the artillery to keep the opposite hills covered with a protective blanket of mist whilst his men stormed across the river? He felt sure it was, for the general in charge of the battle was himself a gunner and knew only too well the value of good artillery support. Every attack that Milne had been through had always been well backed by the field guns in the rear. With smoke to screen the assault and follow-up troops crossing immediately behind them, 'A' Company's task did not, on the face of it, seem too onerous. In the event, it was to be 'A' Company's last attack. By dawn, they had all but ceased to exist.

Across the river, Hauptman Meyer had set out his battle group along the high spur that overlooked the town of Vernon. For the past four days his men had been strengthening the defences along the eastern side of the Seine between Giverny and Vernonnet. Since arriving in the area on 21 August with part of his battalion, Meyer had been expecting the remainder of his men from the 150 Grenadier Regiment to join him at any time. He intended to use them to fill the gap on his left between his present positions and those of the German 18th Air Force Division further up the river. He knew that the reinforcements were on their way and understood why they were taking such time in arriving; any open movement along roads east of the river was often subject to sudden attack by Allied fighter bombers. Most large moves could only be done at night. By the evening of 25 August, the rest of his men had still not arrived at the Seine from Beauvais.

Meyer knew that some Americans had arrived in the town of Vernon on the other side of the river a few days earlier. He also knew that they had moved on down the river valley towards Rouen, leaving just a few reconnaissance troops and artillery observers to stir up the Free French forces that were holed up there. There had been some desultory shelling coming from the far bank earlier that day, just as there had been every other day since the Americans passed by, but by late afternoon everything had settled down. Even the sporadic small arms fire from the French resistants had stopped. His men began to relax; some even sunbathed in the warm evening sunlight.

Although Battle Group Meyer numbered only 148 men, what they lacked in numerical strength was more than made up for by their perfect defensive positions along the high chalk escarpment. Gathering silently opposite, separated only by a few grassy meadows and 680ft (206m) of water, was a whole British infantry division which when complete would number over 14,000 men. However, all this was unknown to Hauptman Meyer – unknown, that is, until the guns opened up.

Chapter 1

Vernon on the Seine

At 0340 hours on 4 June 1940, the old destroyer *Shikari* sailed for England from the besieged port of Dunkirk. On board were the last of the 338,226 men to be evacuated from the town and beaches, all that remained of the British Expeditionary Force. The rapid collapse of the British and French armies, in the face of the blitzkrieg advance of the German armoured forces, had taken only twenty-five days. As the British withdrew to organise the defence of their islands, they left behind a shattered and demoralised French nation. France, alone, was left to stage a last-ditch stand on the line of the Somme and Aisne rivers. It was doomed to failure. On 6 June the line broke and the German panzers raced to the Seine.

Saturday 8 June 1940 was clear and sunny. Life in Vernon began much the same as on any other market day. By half-past nine in the morning, people from the surrounding villages were beginning to gather in the town to buy and sell their produce. Shops were open, children were at school, and the war, despite all the bad news, still seemed remote. It was, however, closer than the citizens of Vernon realised, for a rampaging enemy army was closing rapidly on that peaceful scene and its advance guard was, even at that moment, in the skies overhead.

There was no warning as the German bombs fell on the town. People caught unprotected in the open were easy victims. The raid had no real objectives, save to induce terror in the populace and confusion among the retreating French army. Indiscriminately, the bombs struck home among the streets and buildings. A hairdressing salon here, a small house there; death came by chance. The air raid was swift; in a moment the bombers had gone. Silence and disbelief crept over the town.

At two in the afternoon the planes came back, attacking the Paris–Le Havre railway line. Again at seven in the evening, twenty more aircraft circled the defenceless town, bombing this time with incendiaries as well as high explosives. The fires that started quickly began to spread among the medieval half-timbered houses and, as the night closed in, the flames served to illuminate an escape route for the long line of refugees who quit the town. Sorry groups of frightened people fled to the safety of the Forest of Bizy where, helpless, they looked down on their town burning before them, the red glow reflected in the dark Seine. A fourth raid, the last that day, was a minor affair, a few aircraft serving to kill a solitary old woman.

All night and well into the next day the fires continued to burn. The bombers returned at four o'clock, then again at seven and finally at nine, the pace of the attacks increasing as the enemy's ground forces drew closer. Throughout the day, straggling parties of French soldiers streamed back across the river and through the town, moving westwards away from the Seine. Vernon was left undefended; it was too late to make a stand against the Germans behind the river. At two in the afternoon, the rearguard of the French forces finally blew the stone road bridge and then they too quit the town. Vernon was by then almost empty; most of its inhabitants had fled the still smouldering town.

They came early on 10 June in rubber boats. At five-thirty in the morning, the first Germans paddled their way over the river unopposed. They were soon joined by others who had crossed elsewhere. Before the day was out, a boat bridge had been built. Then the flood began; thousands of Germans poured across the Seine heading south and west, smothering France. It seemed like the end for Vernon. Captured and broken, its subjugation was to last four long years until, on a dusty summer morning, the men of Wessex brought final liberation.

France signed away her sovereignty at Compiègne on 22 June. To add to her humiliation, the armistice was sealed in the same railway carriage in which the German capitulation had taken place in 1918. Soon the occupying forces were issuing proclamations of increasing severity. German rule was to be supreme; German laws would take precedence over French legislation. The French police were to assist the occupation forces to carry out German laws and ordinances. Death was to be the punishment for a whole series of offences against the occupation: sabotage, possession of firearms, listening to foreign broadcasts, giving help to the enemies of Germany, strikes and picketing; the list seemed endless. France had become completely suppressed under the yoke of Nazism.

'At Vernon, in the beginning, relations with the Germans were very correct,' recalls Robert Laurance.

There was a pessimistic feeling pervading the whole country. We could feel hatred for the Germans because they had won, but we also had the same feelings towards those responsible for our own defeat, that is to say the French Government. Then, little by little, everything began to change and the hatred for the Germans intensified.

After the fall of France, most of the population felt that Britain would be the next victim of the German blitzkrieg. It did not seem possible that any nation could resist the Nazi onslaught. The short stretch of sea separating the British Isles from the continent of Europe was all that stood between freedom and tyranny. The English Channel had saved the nation many times in the past, but could it do so now, against an enemy that dominated the land and probably the air as well? One French fourteen-year-old boy, Gabriel Valet, thought so:

I had been evacuated with my family to the region around the Loire valley. We stopped at an hotel, which was quite empty. In the evening I met a German soldier mounting a guard on the road and began talking to him, using a few words of German and French. I asked where he was going next and he replied, 'Now we are going to England.' Laughingly, I told him I was going to give him my name and address and when in London he would be able to send me a postcard. Still laughing, I then asked him if he could swim. 'No,' he answered … 'Ah well,' I said, 'Then I'm never going to receive my postcard!'

There was no invasion of England. The inability of the German Luftwaffe to dominate the sky served to stall Hitler's plans to cross the Channel and he turned his attention towards Russia. This respite allowed Britain to build up her strength and gave some hope to those people suffering in German occupied territories. All over France, patriots gathered in small groups to organise a resistance to the German presence, each one demonstrating, as Robert Laurance remembers, that typically French trait of rebelling against that which is forbidden.

Vernon was an important communications centre on the lower part of the River Seine, a crossing place for both road and rail networks. Although not heavily industrialised, it did have many important factories doing work for the German war effort. In addition, the enemy had both naval and air force headquarters near the town. The resistance movements of the area were encouraged to provide the British with any details about the German occupation that they could gather.

Vernon became a hotbed of resistance. Several independent groups sprang up in the town as the stubborn Norman character of the people asserted itself. Eventually, the groups in the resistance movement belonged either to the 'English', controlled and supplied by London, or 'French' sections.

Many people joined the resistance because of their political affiliations. Robert Laurance was contacted by both the socialists and the freemasons of the resistance. He was a friend of Georges André, the owner of a small bookshop, who was undoubtedly the great resistance leader of the region. In this way, Laurance belonged to both of the resistance factions:

The 'English' group was well implanted in Vernon. There used to be a bistro in the town called 'Le Bon Coin', owned by a Madame Vermelaine. She spoke perfect English, having been once married to an Englishman for a while. After her cafe was destroyed by the bombing in 1940, she transferred her business to another small shop and it was there that we had our general headquarters. Together with a few peaceful friends, she used to receive us on Sundays and we used to play cards and eat well on the black market. When one examines the history of the resistance, one notices the difficulties that existed between the various groups. There was no question of incorporating the English group with the French group, because it was English controlled pure and simple.

Others joined the resistance out of hatred for the Germans, whilst some were forced into it as a result of spontaneous actions. In 1942, Gabriel Valet was in Paris travelling on the Metro:

A German officer wanted to board a train which was full. He tried to throw me out of my seat. I said to him, 'Ah old chap, I am here, at home in my own country', and refused to move. He insisted, so I punched him and threw him off the train! Two men who were watching all this advised me to get off of the train at the next stop, because they were sure I would be picked up somewhere down the line. One of them took me to his house and that was how I joined the resistance.

Valet's Paris group was later decimated when it was denounced to the Gestapo. He avoided capture and moved to Vernon. Like all the members of the resistance, he led a double life. During the daytime he worked in one of the factories, whilst at night he gathered information for the Allies. His work as a storekeeper enabled him to sabotage inflatable boats that were produced for the German Luftwaffe. The Germans would inspect the finished product and then put each boat in store to await despatch. By the time they were taken away and loaded on lorries, Valet had made sure they were full of holes. 'Any shot-down airman using one of my boats would have to quickly learn how to swim, the boats were sure to deflate.'

Not all of the population was sympathetic to the resistance movement's cause. Many collaborated with the Germans, sometimes out of fear, sometimes to gain favour. A few actually enlisted in the German forces and embraced the Nazi philosophy completely. However, the great majority simply wanted to get on with their lives as safely as possible.

'You must not think that people's lives were tragic all the time,' recalls Robert Laurance. 'First of all people were preoccupied with the question of food. Then the difficulty in feeding and clothing oneself, added to all the other worries of all kinds. In the main, people just wanted to get back to normality.' Nevertheless, for those citizens of Vernon who had chosen to defy the occupation forces with acts of resistance, there was to be no normality until the hated Germans had gone.

Mademoiselle Louise Damasse, codename 'Laure', was a young schoolteacher who lived with her mother in the Rue Yvelin. She had joined the resistance because she was already acquainted with other members, notably Georges André. Initially she set up her own group, but later this was joined with a larger cell, with her acting as intermediary. She was given the task of accumulating all kinds of information about German troop movements and activities. This information was gathered in many different ways. People used to bring all kinds of details about the Germans to her house. Here it was collated with news that she had gathered herself and a bulletin was written, which was then taken by her lieutenant to a radio transmitter located in the valley of the River Epte. From there the news was transmitted to England. It was a life filled with danger. The kitchen of her modest home was sometimes filled with the most wanted men of the resistance, as they all met to discuss tactics.

One gets used to danger; one trembles inside, but one gets used to it. One day I was nearly arrested because Georges André had been arrested and the young man who betrayed him betrayed me as well. The bell rang and Madame André was standing on my doorstep. She came to warn me that the Gestapo in Paris knew my name, address and of my activities as a resistance member. So I decided to disappear. I stayed with a good friend in a house near the castle in Vernon. The Gestapo never found me. Looking back on those times, I remember our greatest worry was food; we were always hungry.

Once involved in the resistance, its members lived in perpetual fear of betrayal. Some people were known collaborators and it was possible to keep well clear of them, or at least prevent them from seeing anything suspicious. Sometimes though, the traitors worked alongside resistants in the factories.

Maurice Levoin worked nightshifts in a factory making bullets. He and some of his fellow workers committed numerous acts of sabotage, often dropping pieces of metal into mechanisms so that the machines would have to be taken out of service. In the factory, there was one well-known collaborator. Levoin threatened him with his life if he told the authorities about his activities.

This collaborator lived in a house by the railway track. One night some English aircraft were machine-gunning trains along the Paris–Le Havre railway line. As a result, his house was hit and damaged. The next day, he told us he knew it was us who had told the English about him. He really believed that the English Air Force had organised the raid to attack his house. It was of course pure chance. The poor man still lives in that house.

Often, in the cat and mouse game that went on between the resistance and the Gestapo, people would suddenly disappear. Louis le Maignon and his wife Ezra kept a clandestine radio transmitter hidden in the loft of their house in the Rue St Catherine on the outskirts of Vernon, at Bizy. Twice a week, a man called Charles would come to the house soon after midnight. At 2am he would transmit his messages to London. After he had finished, he left the house and returned to the cemetery where he lodged with the caretaker, a Madame Crecy. The le Maignons never knew anything about the man, he never said a word to them. Then suddenly it ended. They never saw him again; he simply disappeared.

From 1940 until 1944 Vernon carried on as just one of the countless provincial French towns governed by the occupying forces. There were the same acts of sabotage carried out in the vicinity, denunciations, arrests and terror, as were happening in the rest of the country, but Vernon figured no more prominently than any of the other towns of appreciable size in Normandy, save having a reputation for being the location of a strong resistance movement. However, once the Allied planners had decided on Normandy as the site of the invasion, the bridges over the Seine at Vernon began to have a special significance.

All the bridges over the River Seine, between Paris and the sea, had to be cut before the invasion, so as to isolate the area from the east. The stone road bridge at Vernon, destroyed by the retreating French army in 1940, had by that time been repaired by the provision of a metal roadway resting on the old piers. It was a single-track carriageway controlled by traffic lights at either end. Four hundred yards (365m) downstream was an iron-girder rail bridge. This high, single-track bridge was reached by an embankment on both sides of the river.

These two bridges fed a road and rail network that was vital to the German lines of communication. Plans were made for their complete destruction.

In the spring of 1944, the US Ninth Air Force was given the tactical plan for operation 'Overlord', the Allied invasion of France. The first stage was to attack airfields within, or adjacent to, the Normandy invasion area. All airfields in a 130-mile (209km) radius of the assault beaches were neutralised. Between 1 May and 5 June, thirty-six airfields were hit. These attacks ensured that the Luftwaffe was beaten in the air and could not interfere with the coming invasion. Next came the road and rail networks.

Since February, the US Ninth Air Force had been attacking rail installations in northern France: running sheds, marshalling yards, rail centres and locomotive works had all suffered from their medium bombers. Now these attacks increased in frequency and the bombers also turned their attention to the road and rail bridges. On 7 May, the fighter-bombers of the Ninth Air Force attacked the Seine railway bridges at Mantes Gassicourt, Oissel, Orival and Vernon.

Sunday morning of 7 May 1944 was bright and sunny. Maurice Levoin was busy in his allotment near the Forest of Bizy. Around 10am he was disturbed by the noise of a single-engined fighter and looked up to see an aircraft diving straight towards him. The plane then levelled off to pass low over his head at great speed, heading for the railway bridge. Slung beneath it, he could see the outline of two large bombs. No sooner had this plane gone over than another followed, then another and yet another, until a total of eight had passed over in a single line, diving down onto the iron bridge. Seconds later, the bridge was covered with great plumes of water erupting high into the air as the bombs struck home.

One by one, the P-47 Thunderbolts swooped down on the metal spans of the bridge, placing their huge 1,000lb bombs with pinpoint accuracy. Taken by surprise, the German anti-aircraft guns were slow to respond. Before they could effectively interfere with the raid, it was over. Seven of the eight Thunderbolts had bombed the target; the eighth jettisoned its bombs over the town, seemingly in trouble. Then they were gone. The raid was a complete success; when the smoke and spray had cleared their target lay effectively broken, the end of one span tilting uselessly into the Seine.

Most of the massive bombs had found their way to the target, but one errant missile ricocheted off the bridge, then bounced across the island on the far side of the river, slid up the bank and over the Vernonnet–Pressagny road, finally to come to rest, upright, against the side of a house. Thankfully, it proved to be a dud.

One flight of eight Thunderbolts, sixteen 1,000lb bombs and a few minutes of action were needed to sever the Vernon rail bridge. The raid was brilliantly executed and one hundred per cent effective. In comparison, the raid on the road bridge nineteen days later was a messy affair.

On 26 May, the stone road bridge linking Vernon with Vernonnet was attacked by medium bombers from the Ninth Air Force. The B-26 Marauders came in three waves, bombing from high altitude. Unfortunately, they did not achieve the pinpoint accuracy of the dive bombers. The destruction of property in Vernon equalled that done by the Germans in 1940.

At six-thirty in the evening they attacked without warning. The bombs began to burst well back from the river, then gradually crept forward towards the bridge. Some bombers were well clear of the target when they released their load, leaving strings of explosions to rip along the meadows on the eastern side of the river. Other bombs fell into the Seine, sending great fountains of water skywards. The town centre of Vernon was badly hit, as were the houses alongside the Seine. The Americans were using large, high-explosive bombs and their destructive power was terrifying. Buildings were pulverised into rubble, leaving sixty-foot (18m) deep craters.

Fourteen-year-old Guy Dugrès was in the Place Chantrelle with his mother when he heard the bombs falling:

> We flattened ourselves on the ground in the entrance of a house opposite the Hotel Chantrelle. The bombs seemed to land all around us; the hotel was razed to the ground in just a few seconds. We quickly joined the people of the house and sheltered in the cellar. After a few minutes the second wave came over, more bombs and then the third wave arrived. This last wave managed to hit the bridge and then they too were gone. I was very frightened, as was my mother. When we came out of the cellar there were many dead and injured lying in the streets. It was like a lunar landscape, everywhere there was destruction. We then went home quickly and that same evening my mother, who was very shaken by it all, took me away to the country. We did not return until just before the liberation.

The raid was successful in that the bridge had been hit and the first two spans badly damaged, but it was achieved only at great cost to the town and its people. Fifty-two buildings had been destroyed, 150 people were homeless, 35 were injured and no fewer than 47 killed. The Allied liberation of Normandy was beginning to exact a high cost from the inhabitants.

On 6 June, the Allies landed on the coast of Normandy. From that moment, people all over France became impatient to be liberated. There was an upsurge in the numbers of people working for the resistance. Thousands of men flocked to join the underground FFI (French Forces of the Interior). For the whole of June and July, the Allies were confined to the area of Normandy near the beaches, but in August came the breakout and with it hopes in Vernon soared. By the middle of the month, many of the Germans in the town had started pulling out.

Chapter 2

The Allies Move to the River Seine

The Americans were the first to arrive at the River Seine. General George Patton's XV Corps was released from the task of encircling the trapped Germans at Falaise and raced on to the river. On 19 August, its 79th Division arrived at Mantes, an industrial town on the Seine thirty miles (48km) below Paris, and found the place deserted. Just outside the town a patrol found an unguarded catwalk across a ruined dam that was passable to men on foot. The discovery was quickly exploited and within a short time the Americans had a bridgehead over the Seine. It was all so easy; the Germans had left the area to guard the approaches to Paris. No other crossing of the Seine was to be quite so simple.

With the arrival of the Americans on the Seine, it became possible to contemplate a further encirclement of those German forces still west of the river between Paris and the sea, including those that had escaped the Falaise débâcle. There were estimated to be around 75,000 men and 250 tanks trying to retreat to safety across the Seine. General Bradley, Patton's senior, and commander of all the American land forces, now suggested that his troops should drive down the Seine valley, pushing those retreating Germans towards the sea. This move would also capture the numerous rafting sites that were transporting the defeated enemy across the river to safety. Below Rouen, the Seine is tidal and much wider, rendering it extremely difficult for any rafting. If the enemy could be pushed further and further down the valley, it would eventually be trapped against the sea and completely destroyed.

There was, however, a major drawback with such a manoeuvre. The northern stretch of the river below Mantes was in the zone allocated to the British 21st Army Group (First Canadian and Second British Armies). The passage of American troops down the river valley would cut right across the proposed line of advance of the British and Canadian armies – a move that would be likely to cause all kinds of administrative problems. It seemed probable that Montgomery would be appalled at such a suggestion, going, as it did, against his orderly and methodical approach to each advance. The Americans were proposing to move across the front of his two armies at the

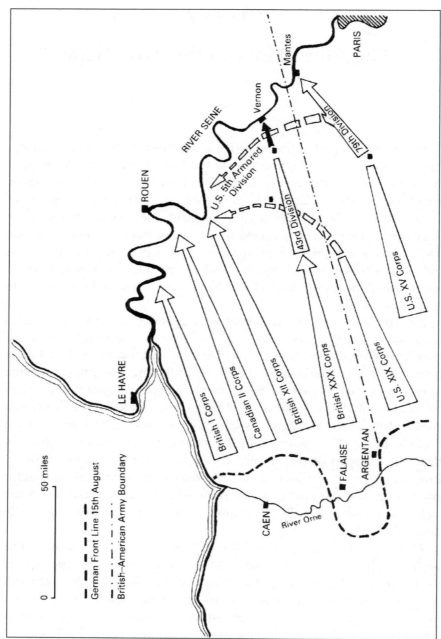

Map 1. Allied drive to the River Seine.

very moment he was organising their greatest leap forward since arriving in France. The whole idea was a contradiction of his intention that his 21st Army Group should reach the Seine with all speed, for all those American troops who marched northwards down the river valley would, eventually, have to march back again, right across the path of the advancing British and Canadians.

Surprisingly, Montgomery agreed to this plan, stating that it would be a good opportunity of finishing the business of clearing the area of Germans in record time. He realised that it would be a good while before his own troops could be ready to move eastwards, for they were still in the process of clearing the remains of the German resistance around Falaise. Indeed, in the north of the area around Caen, some troops were in action against fresh enemy reinforcements brought into the line from the German Fifteenth Army before the main collapse. Montgomery was also pleased with the idea of advancing to the River Seine against negligible resistance, the way having been cleared by the Americans. However, probably the likeliest reason for his agreeing was as a result of the criticism he had received over the length of time it had taken to close the Falaise 'gap', allowing thousands of Germans to escape. He was not about to let another chance of pocketing the retreating enemy evade him.

Hitler was completely out of touch with the enormity of the collapse in Normandy. On the same day that the Americans began their move northward down the Seine valley, the German Commander-in-Chief ordered that a stand be made on the River Touques. This new line was sixty miles (96km) in front of the Seine and had already been outflanked by the Americans. In truth, most of the German survivors from the Normandy battles were attempting to put the greatest possible distance between themselves and the pursuing Allies, their only hope of survival being to get back across the Seine as quickly as possible.

Although the majority of these fleeing German troops had become no more than a rabble, there were some individual officers who had come to terms with the situation. Under their initiative, various battle groups were hastily formed to delay the Allied advance and to buy time for those troops in the process of being ferried to safety at sites around Rouen. By collecting together retreating tanks and passing groups of infantry, they were able to assemble strong pockets of resistance. The Americans did not have to travel far down the Seine valley before they ran into these German battle groups.

The thirty-mile (48km) drive from Mantes to Louviers, made by the US 5th Armored Division, was frequently held up by such actions. As the division came closer to the German ferry sites, so the resistance increased.

The densely wooded valleys provided good cover for small enemy parties to ambush and delay the American tanks, the defenders skilfully using the undulating terrain to their advantage. It took five days before the division finally reached Louviers, and that after much heavy fighting. Those remnants of the Fifth Panzer Army gave a good account of themselves, winning precious time for their comrades who were carrying out the ferrying operations further north around Rouen.

With the final sealing of the Falaise 'gap' on 20 August, the British and Canadian armies were at last able to look to the east and begin the move out of the confines of the close Normandy countryside. However, the northern arm of the pincer movement to close the pocket had left the 21st Army Group with a complicated manoeuvre to perform before its two armies would be facing the Seine.

All the roads in the area were choked by vast traffic jams, made all the worse by the debris strewn around from the shattered German army. The intensity of the fighting in this upper part of the trap would mean that there could be no rapid dash to the River Seine. There were still many German formations between Caen and the lower reaches of the river that had not been caught up in the collapse. Both the Canadian First Army and the British Second Army now began complicated wheeling movements to bring themselves round to face the fleeing enemy and to be ready for the great push to the Seine.

Four of the five corps that comprised the 21st Army Group joined together to advance eastwards on a broad front. The fifth, the British VIII Corps, was kept in reserve at Vire. General Crerar, Commander of the First Canadian Army, sent his I Corps towards Pont Audemer, along the line St Pierre sur Dives–Lisieux–Pont L'Évèque to clear the coast. The Canadian II Corps drove eastwards along the route Vimoutiers–Bernay–Elbeuf to join up with the Americans. The Second British Army, commanded by General Miles Dempsey, had XII Corps heading for Louviers on the Seine. Finally, XXX Corps was assigned the task of advancing along the right-hand boundary between the British and American forces, to reach the Seine at Vernon.

General Dempsey could not readily deploy his Second Army until the Canadians on his left had wheeled northwards to make way for him. This delayed the start of XII Corps' advance, but on the right XXX Corps began picking its way through the devastation around Argentan and sent the British 11th Armoured Division forward on 21 August. Bypassing enemy resistance in Gâcé, the division reached L'Aigle the following day. Next, 50th Division came up on the left and pushed on, arriving in the area Verneuil–Breteuil on

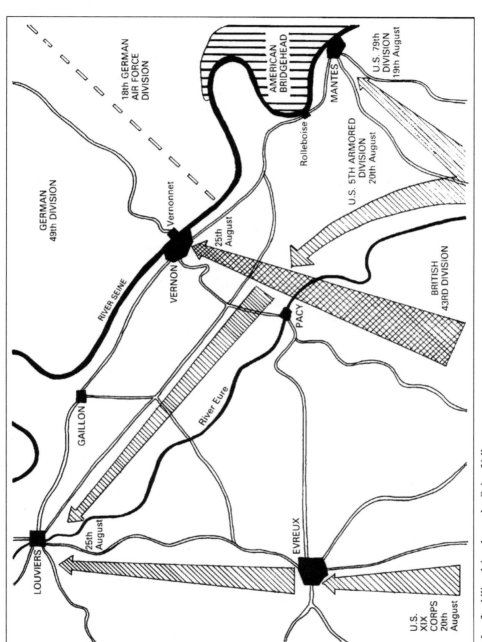

Map 2. Allies drive down the Seine Valley.

23 August. Here it remained, for the way forward was blocked by the American XIX Corps, which had moved across the line of advance and into the British sector on its drive northwards down the Seine.

Since the decision had been made not to halt on the Seine, but to press on over once it had been reached, the river no longer seemed the formidable barrier it once was. Nevertheless, it would still take several major operations to get the two armies across, but the presence of American troops on its eastern bank and the disorganised state of the German army west of the river made it unlikely that the enemy could resist several simultaneous assaults against it. Montgomery now set his sights far beyond the river; he was looking towards Amiens and on into Belgium. If the momentum of the advance could be maintained, allowing the enemy no respite, then an early liberation of the Channel ports could be envisaged, which in turn would lead to an easing of the supply problems. To act as the spearhead for this epic drive into northern France and Belgium, Montgomery had chosen XXX Corps. Commanding this famous corps was a great favourite of Montgomery's, Lieutenant-General Brian Horrocks.

Horrocks was a soldier of exceptional ability, well liked by both officers and men. He was a soldier's soldier. In the words of one of his brigadiers in XXX Corps, Brigadier Essame of 214 Brigade: '... he had perfect manners, a lively sense of humour, good looks and great personal charm. He epitomised every quality the British soldier expects in his leaders in the heat of battle. Men fought for him because they liked him personally and trusted him, because in a crisis they knew he would be with them.'

Horrocks had been a brigade commander in Montgomery's 3rd Division at Dunkirk and went on to command the 9th Armoured Division after a short while in England. He later teamed up again with Montgomery, this time in Egypt, taking charge of first XII Corps, and then X Corps. Whilst in North Africa, he was wounded in an air raid on Bizerta, which resulted in his being invalided back to England. Doctors found his injuries to be serious and Horrocks was told that he would never take command in the field again. There followed fourteen months of hospitalisation, by which time his enormous reserves of will-power and determination had helped him to a remarkable recovery – so much so, that late in July 1944 Montgomery summoned Horrocks across the Channel to join him in France. The battle for Normandy was not going exactly to plan and Montgomery had made some changes in high places. Horrocks was given command of XXX Corps on 3 August. He could not have rejoined the war at a more opportune moment.

By the beginning of August 1944, the blood-letting in Normandy was coming to an end as the hard static fighting neared its climax. It was a time when bold, far-reaching movements could be contemplated by leaders with drive and enthusiasm. The moment called for commanders who were able to exploit the situation with sweeping actions, denying the enemy breathing space to regroup; Horrocks was just such a man.

With the collapse of the German Seventh and Fifth Panzer Armies at Falaise, Horrocks was determined that XXX Corps would make for the Seine and beyond, with all speed. He therefore selected the 43rd (Wessex) Division to carry out an assault across the great river at Vernon, some fifty miles (80km) below Paris. He chose this division for the attack for reasons which he explains in his book *Corps Commander.*

The 43rd (Wessex) Division was an obvious choice for the actual crossing. Its commander, Major–General G.I. Thomas, though a very difficult man, was an immensely able divisional commander, and nobody in the British Army had given more detailed thought into the problem of crossing rivers in the face of opposition. For two–and–a–half years before D–Day he had exercised troops on this most exasperating and complex type of operation, including the crossing of the Medway, the Rother, and the aptly-named Reading Sewer, preferably in the tidal reaches and by night, in heavy rain and mid–winter. With the forcing of the crossing at Vernon, in the teeth of enemy fire, of one of the great rivers of Europe, over 650 feet wide, with a strong current and muddy bottom, his hour was about to come.

At XXX Corps HQ near Moulins-sur-Orne on the evening of 22 August, Major–General Thomas arrived to be given orders for the operation. He was instructed 'to force a crossing of the Seine on or about the 25 August. To cover the construction of a Class 9, a Class 40 and a Class 70 bridge. To form a bridgehead of sufficient depth to allow passage through of the remainder of the Corps.'

The operation called for Thomas to plan and undertake an assault crossing of a wide river against an enemy-held shore, in broad daylight, after an advance of over 120 miles (193km), all within the space of three days. It was a tall order.

Chapter 3

The Plan

The choice of Vernon as the site for XXX Corps' crossing of the Seine was an obvious one. On the section of river assigned to the corps, only at Vernon was there the necessary road network capable of handling the volume of traffic that would have to pass through the bridgehead as the British Second Army pushed on across northern France.

When, on 22 August, Major-General Thomas was given his orders for the assault, his 43rd Division was in the rear of XXX Corps' area around Écouches. The River Seine was over one hundred miles (160km) away. To the troops who had spent the previous two months closely confined in the Normandy 'bocage', where an advance of just a few hundred yards was considered a breakthrough, the whole operation seemed rather fanciful.

Late on 19 August, news filtered through to the people of Vernon that the Americans had arrived on the river at Mantes, some twenty miles (32km) upstream. The next day, the US 5th Armored Division turned north and began to motor down the Seine valley.

By this time, most of the German forces had quit Vernon and withdrawn across the Seine over the partly demolished road bridge that was still usable. During the previous few days there had been a steady stream of retreating enemy troops pulling back across the river, fleeing the advancing Americans. The FFI in Vernon were convinced that freedom was at hand and, under the leadership of Georges André, rose up and liberated themselves. All the resistance men pulled on their FFI armbands and paraded through the streets with their weapons. For the first time in over four years, the French tricolour flew again from public buildings. It was, however, a little premature, for when the leaders of the FFI met with the Americans just outside Vernon, they were told that the town had been assigned to the British, who were at that time still over one hundred miles (160km) away. Other than a few reconnaissance troops, no Americans would be entering the town. By this time, it was too late for the FFI to back down; André decided to hold Vernon until the British arrived.

The first job they tackled was to cut the remains of the stone road bridge, so as to prevent any more Germans coming back over the river. Using some plastic explosives that had been hidden in the woods near Pressagny l'Orgueilleux by a resistant called Louis Neuvilly, they blew the pier that was holding the damaged spans, making the remains impassable.

In the town, the FFI began clearing all the houses of the last few Germans who were in hiding. Most of these unfortunates were trying to stay under cover until the Americans arrived, so that they might desert. They did not want to trust themselves to the French resistance. One fourteen-year-old boy, Guy Dugrès, joined in the hunt with some friends:

> We found a terrified German hiding at the bottom of a well. I had my own machine-gun, although it did not have a breach mechanism and couldn't fire. Anyway, by threatening this soldier with it, we managed to get him out of the well and proudly marched him into Vernon along the Rue de Bizy. One frightened enemy soldier, hands on head, followed by a group of small boys; it made a glorious sight. Then we handed him over to the FFI.

By the end of the day, the French resistants had complete control of the town. They had taken over the barracks and had mounted a guard on the ruins of the old road bridge to stop any enemy infiltration back across the river. Vernon was in their hands, but with only light weapons at their disposal, it was also at the mercy of any large party of Germans who wished to take it back.

The rejoicing in the town was short-lived. As the impatient citizens of Vernon awaited the arrival of the British, with their houses bedecked with flags and a feeling of festivity in the air, three German tanks motored back into the town, retreating from the Americans. However, by this time the FFI had tasted freedom and they were determined to hold on to their new-found liberty; they clashed head on with the tanks.

The commander of one of the tanks was shot dead in front of the town hall. At the same time, a young Frenchman, Pierre Zymslony, threw a grenade into the open turret of the second tank, but before the bomb exploded, the young FFI man was shot dead by a burst of machine-gun fire from the armoured vehicle. The third tank was set on fire and its commander wounded. It was too much for the enemy, who took flight out of the town and down the Seine valley. The confidence of the FFI soared. Now convinced that the Germans were finished, they began offensive operations of their own out of the town, helping the Americans to mop up any isolated enemy soldiers.

For a while, after their local troops had withdrawn, the far side of the river was devoid of any Germans. Then, on 21 August, elements of the German

49th Infantry Division arrived in Vernonnet from Boulogne, to strengthen the line of the river in anticipation of an Allied crossing. This new development was a problem for the FFI in Vernon, for it meant that there was now an enemy presence overlooking the town, from positions just a few hundred yards away across the water. The German soldiers, existing so close to the hot-blooded Frenchmen, proved to be tempting targets. There followed a few days of sporadic small-arms fire across the Seine, as the more volatile FFI members took target practice with any unfortunate German who happened to expose himself. Retaliation came in the form of occasional shells and mortar fire from the enemy positions high on the opposite cliffs.

Louis Le Maignon was placed in one of the houses that lined the road on the Vernon end of the remains of the road bridge, guarding against any German attack across the ruins:

Our group was supposed to have a heavy machine-gun. I spent most of the day carrying ammunition to the basement, only to find out later that there was no machine-gun. I had an automatic rifle, but it seemed to me that I was only there to be shot at. The two men with me had a tommy-gun and another rifle. We tried firing at the Germans a few times, but they never attempted a crossing. The next morning we were relieved and we came back home. My kids asked me if I had killed many Germans. I answered that happily they did not advance, so we did not have to do very much. It was just as well, for we had little ammunition that fitted our guns.

The days passed slowly. A few Americans entered the town but they were either reconnaissance troops or artillery observers. Then, on 24 August, some Americans of a different kind entered the town. Jacques Cambuza watched their arrival with interest:

Two American jeeps pulled into the main square and, although they came with the aim of liberating us, they left me disenchanted. The American jeeps contained soldiers who were specially trained for the job; interpreters who began to lavishly hand out cigarettes. They had a certain aloof look about them, they were not fighting soldiers. They imagined that they could buy us with their gifts. It wasn't very nice.

Then the Americans left. Vernon was still in a state of limbo. Was the town liberated, or not? Would the Germans return, but most of all, where were the British?

When Thomas arrived back at his headquarters from his visit to XXX Corps' commander Brian Horrocks, he spent half-an-hour in his caravan alone, pondering the problem of the crossing. By 2100 hours, he had formulated a plan and quickly summoned to a conference the commanders of the units he had chosen to spearhead the assault.

The general outlined his ideas for the operation, which by this time had been given the codeword 'Neptune'. The assault was to be mounted by 129 Brigade (4th and 5th Wiltshires, and 4th Somerset Light Infantry), reinforced by a battalion from 214 Brigade (1st Worcestershires). The division's own engineers were to build the first bridge, a Class 9 folding boat bridge, immediately after the initial assault, to enable a rapid build-up of troops into the bridgehead. Later, larger bridges capable of carrying tanks were to be erected by other Royal Engineer formations.

For operation 'Neptune' to stand any chance of success, surprise and speed were essential. The division had just three days to plan and execute the crossing. No easy task, for the final plan evolved by Thomas had to be capable of dealing with any unexpected developments. As he disappeared back into his caravan after the 'orders group' meeting, he was heard to remark: 'This is the sort of operation that the Staff College would lay down that a fortnight's planning would be necessary to ensure success. We have got to plan and get it right in a few hours.'

Thomas had every reason to be concerned. For only five days before, Second Army Headquarters had estimated that seven to ten days would be needed to prepare for an opposed crossing. However, during those five days the picture had changed somewhat; the Americans were now on the Seine.

The biggest problem facing the division on its drive to the Seine was a sensitive one. Blocking its way were the lines of communication of the two American corps who were driving down the Seine valley.

To any army engaged in battle, communication lines are a jealously guarded thing. Along these normally inviolable arteries pass all the daily supplies of food, ammunition, petrol and stores needed to keep action at the front sustained. Protocol demands that no one should cross those lines of communication belonging to another without special reason. In this case, it took protracted negotiations, at army level, to secure passage for the British troops along the road east of Breteuil (a route that would have been theirs by right, had not Montgomery decided to allow the Americans to drive north towards Rouen). Movement eastwards at the vital crossroads was sanctioned only at specific times on certain days. There were to be three four-hour periods when the division could use the road: 0800 to 1200, and 1400 to 1800 hours on 25 August and again from 0100 to 0500 hours on 26 August.

The restricted use of the road eastwards added to the immense problems already facing Thomas at his HQ. It would mean that the division would have to be split into three groups to negotiate the last part of the advance to Vernon.

The first group would arrive in the town on the actual day of assault, leaving little time to make any last-minute adjustments to the final plan. The exact composition of this Assault Group would require careful thought, for the group would have to have with it everything necessary to meet with any eventuality. Moreover, what it could contain was limited to that which could be accommodated in 1,800 vehicles (the maximum number that could pass through the checkpoint in the time available). The make-up of the other two groups was equally critical. Their composition depended upon the point at which the units they contained were introduced into the battle.

These immense preparations for the crossing, so full of military imponderables, had now reduced the operation to a study of convoys, traffic plans and timetables. Decisions made during that first night and throughout the next day by the divisional commander and his staff officers were crucial to the outcome of the whole battle. Little by little, the plan for the assault was put together. As each intricate problem arose, a solution was evolved. All manner of possibilities had to be catered for.

It was well known that the American XIX Corps was present in force as far as the River Eure, but between the Eure and the Seine the American 5th Armored Division had met stiff opposition from German units acting as a rear guard. The situation east of Pacy on the Eure was vague, with the enemy still thought to be active in the area. This lack of information as to what was happening to the north of the route to Vernon dictated that the left flank of the advance would need special protection. The town of Vernon itself would also need to be defended, so as to provide a firm base from which the attack would take place. Therefore, one of the battalions that had been earmarked for the assault (4th Wiltshires) was now given the task of controlling the town immediately on arrival. The Wiltshires were to be assisted in holding Vernon by a squadron of tanks from 15th/19th King's Royal Hussars. More tanks from this regiment were to provide a defensive stop-line to the north of the town, in case the enemy tried to interfere with the crossing. Further afield, the 43rd Reconnaissance Regiment would carry out fighting patrols and try to determine the enemy's intentions.

In committing the 4th Wiltshires to the defence of Vernon in the initial stages, only three battalions were left to carry out the attack across the river. This shortage of infantry dictated that the initial bridgehead would be small and concentrated around the proposed bridging sites. As speed was an important factor, the new bridges would have to be erected close to the demolished road bridge and make use of the existing approaches.

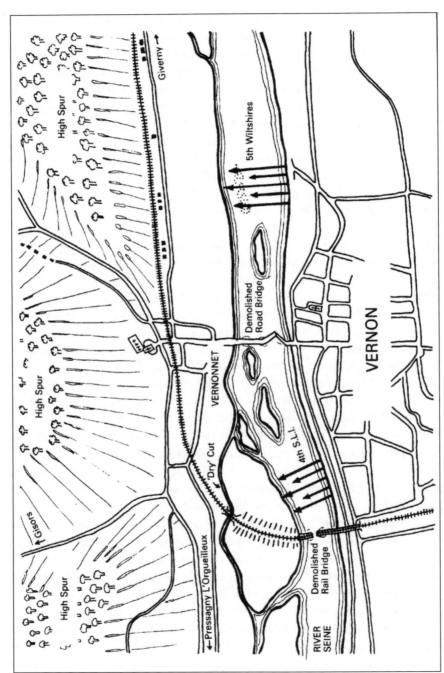

Map 3. Plan of attack.

On the far bank, the village of Vernonnet was clustered around the exit of the old road bridge. Ideally this would be the spot to land, so that the bridging sites could be quickly secured and building could begin at once. However, to land there would present the assaulting infantry with the immediate problem of clearing the village; an operation that could easily lead to delays and heavy casualties from fighting in narrow streets along the river bank.

The final plan therefore decided that the assault would go ahead on a two-battalion front, one on either side of Vernonnet and then, after each battalion had established itself on the far side, they would move along the river bank to clear the village and the bridging sites.

Along the River Seine in the vicinity of Vernon there are many islands of varying sizes dotted about in the fast-flowing current. Four hundred yards below Vernonnet is a large island close to the eastern shore. The railway line that once linked Vernon and Vernonnet crossed this island after it had reached the far side of the river via the demolished iron-girder rail bridge. The line then continued on an embankment before it finally reached the mainland over a small bridge. With the limited resources available to the staff at divisional HQ, it was difficult to decide whether this broad cut separating the island from the mainland was wet or dry.

Usually a stereoscopic pair of air photographs would allow the Army Photographic Intelligence Section representative at divisional HQ to make a definite decision on matters such as this. Unfortunately, there was only a single air reconnaissance photograph available. From this one picture, the photo-reconnaissance expert formed the opinion that the cut was probably dry and shingly, with only a trickle of water in the middle. Passage over for troops would be possible and the island was therefore selected as the landing site for the left-hand assault to be carried out by the 4th Somerset Light Infantry – it was a decision that was to have unfortunate consequences during the attack.

Upstream of the demolished road bridge was another island in mid-river and immediately above that was a very shallow section of river; the resulting ripples on the surface of the water could be clearly seen in the air reconnaissance photograph. The river here was ideal for a crossing. There were good approaches to the near bank and wide grassy meadows on the far side, almost perfect for a landing place. To attempt a crossing below the island would bring the assaulting infantry too close to the village of Vernonnet, whilst to cross further upstream of the shallows would probably push them too far out.

With these thoughts in mind, Thomas provisionally decided that the right-hand assault by the 5th Wiltshires would take place in this vicinity, with the boats passing over the submerged island, unless on-the-spot reconnaissance showed there to be insufficient depth of water to allow their safe passage. It was also decided that the follow-up battalion, the 1st Worcestershires, should be passed over there at the same point.

For the assault itself, there were three types of craft available to the Royal Engineers to carry the attacking infantry across: collapsible canvas assault boats powered by paddles, plywood stormboats powered by motors, and DUKWs (amphibious lorries). The great width and fast-flowing current of the Seine precluded the use of the flimsy assault boats and so the main choice lay between the stormboats and the DUKWs.

The amphibious DUKWs were capable of carrying troops on the journey to Vernon, so that with infantry loaded and ready for action, they could be launched immediately on arrival. They did, however, need a gently sloping river bank from which to launch. Intelligence suggested that such conditions existed at Vernon and orders were given for their use, with stormboats to be kept in reserve for ferrying operations. With the three infantry battalions which were taking part in the assault travelling forward in DUKWs, great savings could be made in road space.

The question of available road space in the assault convoy limited the amount of artillery available to the leading group to just one field regiment, containing twenty-four guns. This number was woefully short of the normal artillery backing for an infantry attack, but Thomas expected to have his second group of vehicles, containing the remainder of the field guns together with a regiment of medium artillery, up at the river in time to support the attack.

These decisions having been made, the composition of the vitally important assault convoy could now be formulated. The final grouping was as follows:

Group 1
Squadron of 43rd Reconnaissance Regiment
Squadron of 15/19th King's Royal Hussars Reconnaissance parties
4th Wiltshire Battalion group
5th Wiltshire Battalion group
4th Somerset Light Infantry Battalion group
1st Worcestershire Battalion group
94th Field Regiment Royal Artillery
129 Brigade HQ
43rd Division Tactical HQ
Royal Engineers Group

Chapter 4

Preparations Continue

Throughout the night of 22 August and all through 23 August the planning for 'Neptune' continued. The frenzied activity of headquarters staff was in marked contrast to that of the enlisted men, who were now enjoying a comfortable idleness in the various peaceful, sleepy Normandy villages.

Since coming out of the line on 17 August, the troops had taken full advantage of the respite from the fighting. Parties of men were sent back down the line to the XXX Corps rest camp, near Bayeux, on forty-eight hours' leave. Cinema shows and concert parties were arranged, baths were laid on and for a short while thoughts of war could be put from their minds. A single entry in the diary of Major Algy Grubb of the 1st Worcestershires sums up his feelings at being released from the horrors of the last two months: 'Heaven.'

One of the biggest problems that Thomas and his staff had to wrestle with when planning the operation was the question of supplies. Once the division had arrived in Vernon, it would be 120 miles (193km) from the nearest source of any replenishment. Therefore, the division would have to carry forward with it extra quantities of petrol, rations and ammunition, so as to sustain itself in action until the remainder of XXX Corps caught up. To complicate matters further, as the three groups were to be separated by at least four hours, each party would be isolated from the next and, with restrictions on the use of the road in the American sector, no replenishment either forward or backward could be expected until the whole division had concentrated in Vernon. By that time, the battle would be well under way. As a result, each of the three groups would have to be self-contained, carrying its own reserve supplies.

Composite ration packs (compo rations) for eight days were to be carried by each man in the division. For the motor vehicles, in addition to their normal issue of seventy-five miles worth of petrol, they were ordered to take extra fuel for a further 120 miles. The field guns were supplied with double the usual amount of ammunition, whilst the mortars had three times their normal supply, with a higher than usual proportion of smoke shells. The fact that the division was reinforced by three regiments of tanks, one medium

regiment of artillery and nearly 900 vehicles belonging to other Royal
Engineer groups all added to the logistical problems at HQ.

Reinforcements began to arrive to help make up the losses suffered since
the division's arrival in France. The fighting in Normandy had been very
costly for the British and Canadian armies. The total casualties amounted to
over 70,000 men and after five years of war there was a crisis in the supply of
fighting men. To help replenish the lack of infantry among the various units,
the 59th Infantry Division was disbanded in August and its men sent to
supplement other divisions; some of them were posted to the 43rd Division.

By 23 August, the countryside around Écouches began to fill with men
and equipment ready for the move. From supply depots all over Normandy,
materials started to concentrate in the area assigned to the division:
stormboats and DUKWs from the rear maintenance area just off the beaches
at Arromanches, bridging columns from the vast Royal Engineers' dump
near Bayeux, earth-movers, lorries filled with rubble, cranes, bulldozers and
countless other stores, all of which had been stockpiled weeks before in
preparation for the assault on the Seine.

For an operation such as this, various other specialised corps and army
units would be assigned to individual divisions to supplement their
manpower. So it was for operation 'Neptune', and the 43rd Division took
command of not only more engineers but also a whole armoured brigade,
extra artillery, more RASC vehicles and, most depressing of all, for there
were bound to be casualties, extra medical facilities.

One such unit was the 49th Field Surgical Unit, which was attached to
129 Field Ambulance and was part of the leading brigade. The surgical unit
acted as a mobile operating team, being sent forward close to the action when
casualties were expected. Dr G.L. Haines was an anaesthetist with the unit
and remembers being ordered to the brigade HQ to attend a briefing.

He was told of the great advance that the division was about to undertake
and that they would be more than a hundred miles ahead of any
reinforcements if anything should go wrong. There was a real possibility that
the division could be cut off by the enemy, but should this happen it was vital
that the bridgehead was held until the rest of XXX Corps arrived. It all
sounded to Dr Haines rather like a great adventure.

The battle for the Seine crossing was to comprise two important
objectives. Initially, the infantry were required to make the assault across the
river and establish a bridgehead on the far shore. Then, once this lodgement
had been gained, the second phase in the operation could begin: the building
of the bridges by the Royal Engineers. The early completion of these bridges
was absolutely vital to the success of the whole venture.

Although the Seine was the first great barrier confronting the British after the landings in France, the problems involved in attempting to cross such rivers had been recognised since long before the invasion. From an engineering point of view, the route from the Normandy beaches to Berlin was barred by many wide rivers. The retreating enemy would, in all probability, destroy every bridge and establish defensive moats behind all of these waterways. Most of the rivers might well have to be taken by assault. Then rafts would have to be constructed to carry supplies over and eventually the new bridges built. The scale of the engineering operations was enormous.

Each division had its own engineers who could deal with light bridges, but the larger types needed skills and techniques of a more intricate nature. To cope with these more complex tasks, special Royal Engineer units were formed and were assigned to various corps and armies, to be used where necessary. Three such formations were allocated to the 43rd Division for the Seine crossings: 7th Army Troops Royal Engineers, 15th (Kent) GHQ Troops Royal Engineers and the XXX Corps Royal Engineers.

At that time, the Royal Engineers had two main types of bridge available to them for crossing large rivers: Bailey and folding boat.

The British Bailey bridge had a well-deserved reputation as the most versatile military bridge in the world. In its most simple form it could carry 40 ton loads. Further reinforcing made it capable of handling loads up to 100 tons. As a fixed bridge it had a maximum span of 220ft (66m), but when laid on 60ft (18m) pontoons it could match the width of any river in Europe. The 7th Army Troops Royal Engineers, under the command of Lieutenant-Colonel Tom Lloyd, were given the job of erecting the first 40 ton Bailey across the Seine.

The other type of river bridge was the folding boat bridge. This was a much more simple affair than the Bailey, consisting of lengths of roadway bolted to collapsible boats. As such it was only capable of carrying loads of up to nine tons. Its main virtue was the relative speed with which it could be assembled. It could also be erected by any divisional engineers. The first bridge across the Seine was to be one of these nine-ton folding boat bridges and the 43rd Division's own engineers had been allotted the task of building it.

The need for special skills other than bridge building during a river crossing led to several Royal Engineer formations being trained in the art of watermanship. They were to become proficient in rafting and boating, with a view to assaulting wide, swift rivers, such as the Seine. One such formation was the 15th (Kent) GHQ Troops Royal Engineers, led by Lieutenant-

Colonel Fayle. At the time of the Vernon operation they were masters in the art, but it had not always been so.

On a damp, chilly day in March 1943, Fayle was demonstrating the rafting of a Valentine tank across a lake about 150 yards (136m) wide, to an army commander and his chief engineer. The raft consisted of a section of Bailey bridge and six pontoons, being hauled across the lake by a party of men using a cable. Assisting them were two outboard motors on the raft operated by the crew. The results were not impressive.

It was a slow, laborious task as the unwieldy craft swung from side to side, with each motor in turn pushing the raft out of line. The high-ranking officers were not convinced of the efficiency of the method used. Fayle agreed with them; there had to be a better way.

He could see that cables were not the answer. When one of these rafts was used on a large, fast-flowing river, it would take power to control it – lots of power. Four propulsion units would be needed to give such power, but this of course had been tried many times before. Everyone had witnessed the uncontrollable yawing that followed when one of the four engines ran slightly faster and swung the raft out of line, followed by frantic efforts to correct the error. The wild gyrations that then occurred were commonplace. Fayle decided to settle on a new approach.

After much deliberation, he reasoned that if an engine was put on each of the outer corners of the raft and the crews pointed these power units along a line of neutral axis (that is, an imaginary line drawn between the motor and the centre of the raft) with the two engines at the front pulling and the two at the rear pushing, there would be much better control over the steering. To turn the craft, the propellers would be swung to the left or the right of the neutral axis, with the pulling and pushing motors acting in an opposite sense. This would swing the raft in the required direction. It would even be possible to move the craft sideways, by reversing the direction of thrust of the two opposing motors.

When Fayle had finally worked out all the details of his scheme, he put his ideas to each of his companies. They were very sceptical; most thought the method was nonsense. Undaunted, Fayle decided to go ahead with a practical demonstration, using one propulsion unit on a Class 40 raft and operating it himself. All his officers and NCOs down to corporal lined the quay to watch their commander make a fool of himself.

To every man there happens, albeit rarely, a day when things quite definitely go right – a day when luck smiles on the fortunate. That morning, on the tidal reaches of the River Quoile in Northern Ireland, there happened just such a day for Lieutenant-Colonel Fayle.

The raft was cast off and the commander pulled his vessel smoothly away from the quay without a scrape. He then proceeded to pilot the craft dead straight along each part of a three-legged course, rounding the two marker buoys with clean, economical turns, and then pulled up smartly back alongside the quay, stopping just three inches from the edge. If he had tried a hundred times, he could never have done it so well again. Elated with his success, he jumped off the craft and turned nonchalantly to the assembled spectators. 'Now go and do likewise,' he snapped. A sheer fluke perhaps, but each man watching was convinced, their scepticism melting away. Every junior officer standing on that quay became fired with a desire to emulate, or even surpass, the proficiency of their commander. Over the following weeks they worked non-stop to perfect this new technique at rafting. The 15th (Kent) GHQ Troops Royal Engineers were on their way to becoming a rafting unit par excellence.

In addition to their rafting skills, the formation went on to perfect their boat handling. The two types of assault craft available to the Royal Engineers at that time were Mark III assault boats (small paddle-powered craft) and stormboats (much heavier plywood boats powered by Evinrude 50HP outboard motors). The unit became proficient in handling both.

As the training progressed, Fayle found that, although his three field companies could handle both rafts and boats, each company had evolved methods of its own that made it more efficient at one particular task. Consequently, by the time the formation was ready to leave for France, 583 Field Company had become specialists in the handling of stormboats and 582 and 584 Field Companies were the complete experts in rafting.

With so much expertise in crossing techniques at their disposal, it was not surprising that Fayle's 15th (Kent) GHQ Troops Royal Engineers were selected for the Seine operation. The unit was earmarked to man the DUKWs during the initial assault and to operate the close support rafts that would be needed on the river before the first bridge opened. Then, after these jobs were over and the 40-ton Bailey had been completed, they were to build a 70-ton Bailey to enable fully loaded tank transporters to cross the river.

The third specialist group of Royal Engineers assigned to the 43rd Division for the battle was the XXX Corps Royal Engineers. Their task in operation 'Neptune' was to provide extra help for any unforeseen events during the long drive to the river. Between the division's present positions and the Seine lay 120 miles (193km) of open road and a number of small bridges. With the tactical situation and the state of the route ahead not completely clear to him, Thomas chose to have with him as many engineers as possible.

Chapter 5

The Move to the Seine Begins

By 24 August, preparations for the great move were complete. In the early hours of an overcast summer's day, the long drive to Vernon began. From their concentration area around Écouches, the first group of vehicles that made up the Assault Group swung north towards Argentan, heading for those places that had seen the worst of the destruction during the encirclement of the German Seventh and Fifth Panzer Armies. The site of the battle presented the onlooker with a scene of complete devastation: mile after mile of burned-out vehicles, tanks and armoured cars reduced to charred shells, guns and limbers twisted into grotesque shapes and everywhere a smell of death. Bloated carcasses of horses, still harnessed to overturned wagons, lay alongside rows and rows of dead men. In every lane and village, piles of smashed and broken refuse gave witness to the defeat the enemy had suffered. In the words of the Allied Supreme Commander, General Eisenhower: 'It was literally possible to walk for hundreds of yards at a time stepping on nothing but dead and decaying flesh.'

During the closing of this 'Falaise pocket', the infantry of the 43rd Division had not been used in the fighting. However, its artillery, along with that of other divisions, was used. The combined guns put down a tremendous barrage on the trapped enemy. Sergeant Sam Beard, a gunner with the 179th Field Regiment RA, can remember his gun firing over 600 rounds of high explosive into the pocket in just one day:

The observation and reconnaissance vehicles returning to our lines were washed down with disinfectant to remove human and animal debris from them. Dead friend and foe alike – for there were many French civilians trapped in the area – lay in heaps, their bodies mixed together with horses and domestic animals, filling the sunken lanes where they had sought shelter. So intense was the carnage of man and beast that all the dead animals could not be buried and later these piles of rotting flesh were bulldozed into heaps and set on fire with petrol.

As the column picked its way through the wreckage around Argentan, the troops could see for themselves that the savage fighting they had been forced to endure in Normandy had at last brought them some sort of victory. To the Wessexmen, the scenes of terrible devastation convinced them that the German army was heading for defeat. Now it was the turn of the British to go 'swanning' through France as conquering heroes.

Once clear of all the chaos and traffic jams near the scene of the German collapse, the division's leading group began to pick up speed. Leading the way at the front of the Assault Group were two squadrons of armoured cars from the reconnaissance regiment. The column sped forward, heading for the final concentration area along open roads reserved for its exclusive use. It was a glorious advance: all along the route cheering crowds welcomed them through each village. The lines of vehicles soon reached towns that had seen none of the destruction so common elsewhere in Normandy, towns where liberation had been swift and painless for the excited French people. They showed their joy by pressing wine and flowers into the hands of the passing troops, sometimes slowing progress almost to a halt.

Sergeant George Drake of the reconnaissance regiment remembers the welcome given to his armoured car and the genuine hospitality of the French civilians everywhere they went. They all wanted the liberators to join them in a celebration drink of the very potent local apple brandy. As Drake recalls:

There seemed to be a great deal of Calvados in every village, enough to fuel a rocket to the moon. It was very powerful stuff. To save offending them, we had a drill in our car – I received the bottle and took a very small nip, then passed it inside to my crew, Bill and Norman. By Norman's feet was a drain plug, through which he used to pour a fair whack of this firewater. When I returned the bottle to the owner he must have thought that the British had asbestos sponges inside them!

The route took the division through Exèmes, Gâcé, L'Aigle and Rugles. By late afternoon the leading troops had reached the final staging area west of Breteuil. Here the convoy pulled off the road to rest for the night. The roads east of Breteuil were reserved for the Americans and were not available to the division until the allotted time the next day.

Between Breteuil and Vernon, 40 miles (64km) away, lay the town of Pacy on the River Eure. At the time when the Assault Group left Écouches, no information was available to them about the vital road bridge across the river at Pacy, although it was known that the Americans were present in the town. However, the American troops were moving down the river valley, not crossing it at right angles as the 43rd Division was hoping to do. This east–west bridge across the Eure therefore was not as vital to their advance as it was to the British and the chances were that it had been demolished.

To clarify the situation at Pacy, a reconnaissance party of Royal Engineers, protected by some armoured cars, slipped through the American checkpoint and went forward to survey the Eure. If the bridge was intact, they were to send a dispatch rider back to divisional HQ with the news and then the survey party was to proceed to Vernon and reconnoitre the near bank of the Seine, thus saving time on the morrow. If the bridge was blown, they were to determine: (a) was it repairable with mobile equipment? (b) if not, was there an alternative site? and (c) what was the length of the gap? To cover the eventuality of the bridge being blown, one set of Bailey bridging equipment for the Eure had been included in the Assault Group.

Number 9 Troop of the 43rd Reconnaissance Regiment led the engineering survey party as they set off to investigate the remainder of the route to Vernon. They filtered through the American checkpoint without any hold-ups and set off on the thirty odd miles to Pacy. There were no problems until they arrived just short of the town at a place called St Acquilin. The road here was a mass of craters, with a road block of burnt-out vehicles barring their way. Suspicious of the blockage, the armoured cars and half-tracks pulled off the road and took to the fields to bypass the potential trap.

In Pacy there was no sign of the enemy, or the Americans. The survey party made straight for the river running through the centre of the town and found the bridge was down, blown by the fleeing enemy. FFI informers gave more depressing news; a rail bridge on the Vernon side of the town was also gone. The dispatch rider was immediately sent back to Breteuil with this news.

Thomas was the kind of general who was always anxious to keep in touch with the ever-changing events at the sharp end. Never one to sit back and wait for news, he ranged far and wide to see for himself any problems that could affect his meticulous plans. This was much to the annoyance of his exasperated HQ staff, who were sometimes completely in the dark about any changes of plan he made whilst at the front.

By early evening, Thomas, his ADC Lieutenant Pat Spencer Moore and his driver had arrived on the banks of the Eure in Pacy. They were met by the sole American representative in the area, a US military policeman. Thomas decided that the river must be bridged at once and, although arrangements to do so were already in hand with the Royal Engineers, he travelled back towards the rest of the division at Breteuil to get things speeded up. He had not gone far when he came upon some of the 43rd's own engineers from 260 Field Company.

Sergeant Pat Tucker had stopped his half-track in the road and was having a chat with a friend of his, Sergeant Alan Moore. To his great surprise he saw, coming from the direction of the enemy, the familiar sight of the divisional commander in his scout car. There were no signs of any other people around, civilian or army.

'Ah, sappers!' exclaimed the general. 'Just the chaps I want. There's a blown bridge a few miles down the road. Will you go up and deal with it?'

'Yes, sir,' replied Tucker. 'But what's the tactical situation up there?' – mindful as he was of the fact that they were well ahead of the rest of the division.

'Oh, there are a few Huns about, but they are very inoffensive Huns' was the general's reply, and off he went.

Tucker and Moore decided to toss a coin to see who should go and check out the bridge. Tucker lost and set off with his driver Private Bullus to have a look.

They arrived in the small town to find the river obstacle surrounded by a party of American engineers, all intent on doing their own survey of the site. The Americans insisted that they were going to build a timber trestle bridge over the river. Thankful that he would not be involved in the operation, Sergeant Tucker expressed to the Americans the gratitude of the British army and returned to his company, which was by this time dealing with some craters further back down the road, leaving the Americans to their work.

Major-General Thomas's habit of being well forward with his leading troops could have come to a disastrous end during the drive to the Seine. Sergeant George Drake's troop was part of 'C Squadron of the 43rd Reconnaissance Regiment. The armoured cars were moving tactically, that is in bounds, and Drake's car was in the lead:

We had just passed some dead-beat American troops by the side of the road, when I spotted a vehicle approaching from the right along a lateral road. I immediately radioed a sighting to the rest of the troop (Able 3–contact–out). On hearing this signal, no one makes any calls until the original caller has come back on the air again to report what he has seen, or done. My next move was to get into a good firing position, which in this case was behind a convenient roadside tree. I am happy to say that we were issued with very good binoculars, because as the vehicle came closer I was able to ascertain that it was neither German nor American, but British. I could also see that the passenger had on a red general's hat!

All the while, the 37mm gun on Drake's armoured car was trained on the general. Just one word from Drake would have been sufficient to immediately enhance the promotion prospects of some brigadier. What followed next was pure pantomime, as Drake tried hard to explain over the air that he had in his sights a Very Important Person, without telling the whole world that the divisional commander was roaming around unprotected. Thomas and his party travelled on oblivious to the whole incident.

At that time, Thomas was looking for the divisional HQ belonging to the American troops in the area. He was anxious to find out the enemy's exact whereabouts between there and the Seine. The Americans had been in the region for several days and were expecting the British eventually to take over control of the area.

Pat Spencer Moore found direction signs to an American unit by the side of a road junction and directed the general's driver to take the car up a lane to the entrance of the divisional HQ. Parked by the side of the road was a jeep with two battle-weary Yanks stretched out, their feet resting on the windscreen and their helmets slipped down over their eyes. As the British scout car drove up to them, one of them straightened up, spat on the ground and exclaimed, 'Jeez, the Limeys have got here at last!'

The news at the American HQ was good: around Pacy the enemy had not been seen for several days, most of the German stragglers had been rounded up, or had fled northwards towards Rouen. Between Pacy and Vernon there had been fighting but the route was now clear. The only hold-up that threatened the operation's timetable was the broken bridge at Pacy.

When the news of the blown bridges arrived at the 43rd Division's tactical HQ at Breteuil, the commander of the 43rd's Royal Engineers, Lieutenant-Colonel Evill, ordered the division's 553 Field Company and the bridging platoon forward to deal with them and the road block at St Acquilin. The 553 Field Company had been reserved for the building of the first bridge across the Seine at Vernon. Unfortunately, this work at Pacy, if undertaken by them, would result in an exhausted company before the main operation had begun. Realising this, the overall commander of the Royal Engineers' operations, Brigadier Davey, ordered 11 Field Company from XXX Corps to be sent to carry out the work.

The engineers from XXX Corps were the first to arrive at St Acquilin and immediately began work on clearing the road block. Tragically, the obstacle was booby-trapped. A tremendous explosion tore through the pile of burnt-out vehicles, sending metal and debris high into the air. Five sappers were lost in the blast. The battle for the Seine bridgehead had claimed its first casualties.

The survey party from the 553 Field Company bypassed the sorry scene at St Acquilin and pressed on into Pacy on foot. At the river, they found the American engineers seen by Sergeant Tucker earlier in the evening intent on erecting their trestle bridge. A discussion ensued between the British engineers' officer and his American counterpart on the opposite bank, as to what was the most effective course of action. An international compromise was reached: the British would build a Bailey bridge across the River Eure, whilst the Americans would deal with the damaged road bridge over the railway.

Chapter 6

The German 49th Infantry Division

Forty miles (64km) to the east of the Wessex Division's staging area around Breteuil was the River Seine. Whilst the British division rested, gathering strength before the next day's battle, its adversary, the German 49th Division, held the line of the river oblivious to the impending attack.

The German 49th Infantry Division was commanded by 54-year-old Generallieutnant Sigfried Macholtz. His division was, on paper at least, a normal Wehrmacht field division. It consisted of three infantry regiments (148, 149 and 150) each containing two battalions, an artillery regiment (Artillery Regiment 149) and the 149 Fusilier Battalion (this battalion was like a British reconnaissance battalion, but was in fact more of a mobile reserve, with mechanised heavy weapons and anti-tank guns).

The 49th Infantry Division was originally formed as the 191st Training Division. It spent the early part of the war in Belgium as a mobilisation and training division. After a spell in southern France in 1943, the division moved back north to the area Montreuil–Etaples–Boulogne, in a coast defence and draft finding role. In the spring of 1944, it was converted to a field division and renumbered as the 49th Infantry Division.

For the next few months it remained in the vicinity of Boulogne as part of the German Fifteenth Army, helping to strengthen Hitler's Atlantic Wall against attack. When the invasion came, it was not in the Pas de Calais area as Hitler had expected, but in Normandy. Nevertheless, Hitler was convinced that the Allies would at some time attack across the narrow stretch of water opposite Dover. He felt that the landings in Normandy were merely a diversionary tactic which preceded a much greater assault. During the whole of June and most of July, whilst the tide of battle in Normandy gradually began to swing against him, Hitler left the Fifteenth Army in place ready to deal with a new Allied landing. It was not until much later that he realised such an invasion was not set to happen.

As the ferocity of the German struggle against the Allied landings increased, so the strength of the 49th Division declined. Macholtz was compelled to provide help to the beleaguered Seventh Army in Normandy. At first the requirement was for men but, as the war of attrition continued, artillery, mortars, heavy machine-guns and transport were all taken from the division and fed into the maelstrom that was Normandy. For replacements, Macholtz in return received groups of conscripted foreigners and immature Hitler Youth. When, at last, the call came for the 49th Division to move from the Pas de Calais and join the front line, it advanced not as a well-trained, well-equipped, fresh division, but as a sadly depleted collection of men from various countries, poorly armed and each having varying degrees of commitment.

On 19 August, the 49th Division was transferred from the Fifteenth Army to the Fifth Panzer Army and dispatched to Beauvais. News of the German collapse in Normandy had meant that the unbridged River Seine now became an important means of slowing down the Allies' drive across northern France towards Germany. General Macholtz was ordered to hold the river between Giverny and Les Andelys and to prevent any crossings. Along that part of the Seine the likeliest target was Vernon and its road network.

On 20 August, the 49th Division set up its headquarters in Beauvais. Macholtz quickly formed a battle group from those men of the 150 Regiment that had arrived in the town and sent them on to the river under the command of Hauptman Meyer. The general intended to reinforce them just as soon as the rest of the division had made the journey from the Pas de Calais area.

Unfortunately, on the previous day the Americans had struck across the Seine at Mantes and the need to contain that crossing dictated that the division's next arrivals went to help the 18th German Air Force Division, who were trying to stifle the expansion of the American bridgehead. In the following few days, the remaining units from the 49th Division began to trickle into Beauvais on an assortment of lorries, captured American trucks and push bikes. Some of them were sent on to the river, whilst others were held in reserve until the American intentions were made clear.

Macholtz knew that for any Allied crossing on his section of the river to be successfully exploited, the attack had to be made close to Vernon. This made its defence much easier to organise, which was just as well considering the small number of troops he had available. The key to such a defensive line would be the exploitation of the high ground on his side of the river.

Along the Seine opposite Vernon are three high spurs: one behind Vernonnet and one on either side of the village. It was on the spur upstream of Vernonnet that Hauptman Meyer set out his battle group. This long escarpment completely overlooked the river-front of Vernon. It was a relatively simple matter for Meyer to organise machine-gun emplacements and establish small cannon covering the water so as to produce a formidably strong position. This policy was repeated on the escarpment downstream of Vernonnet to cover the sites of the demolished road and rail bridges.

By 23 August the defence of the line of the river opposite Vernon had been organised. There were still relatively few German troops in the area, but those that were present totally dominated the scene. German intelligence knew that the Americans had arrived in Vernon and also knew that they had merely passed through the town, sending their main forces on down the river valley towards Rouen. All indications were that there was unlikely to be an attempt at crossing in that area.

The next two days slipped idly by with little action seen or heard. Some desultory shelling took place from time to time and the Free French over the river caused the Germans some irritation with their sniping, but the main threat to the division was the possibility of being outflanked by the Americans who had already crossed upstream. By 24 August, the time was rapidly approaching when the 49th Division would have to be pulled back to help defend the River Somme. It seemed increasingly unlikely that the division would fight its first action of the war here on the Seine.

Chapter 7

The Arrival

To an onlooker, the staging area west of Breteuil presented a most incongruous sight. Among the peaceful orchards and fields, tucked into every farmyard and meadow and completely at odds with the pastoral Norman scene, were the 1,600 vehicles of the division's Assault Group. The drab camouflaged trucks provided a stark contrast to the trees and hedgerows now in full bloom. The earlier overcast sky had at last given way to a beautiful summer's evening.

With the war seemingly miles away, the troops lounged around in small groups enjoying the blissful pastime of doing precisely nothing. It was a time for reliving past battles, remembering fallen comrades and dreaming of home. The prevailing feeling among the men was that the enemy was near to collapse. Jerry was on the run and would not stop until he had reached the Fatherland. This opinion was not, however, shared by everyone.

Private Fred Greenwood was a signaller attached to the 5th Wiltshires. He had joined the battalion a few days previously when his unit, the 5th Battalion Royal Berkshire Regiment, was disbanded. He was a veteran of the D-Day landings and was rather perturbed by the conversation he overheard that evening in a tent full of officers:

They seemed to think that the crossing was going to be a piece of cake. The enemy was supposed to be very weak along the Seine, consisting of old men and those unfit for front line duty. We were going to dash across the river with no trouble at all. It worried me to hear them talk about the coming battle as though it was just a game.

Greenwood left that tent a very sober man. He had a premonition that something was going to happen to him. Later, by the light of a hurricane lamp, he wrote a letter to his fiancée, Iris, back in England. He explained that she might not be hearing from him for some time, but not to worry. He was sure that the next day would change his life, although he was equally sure that he was not about to die. Within the next thirty-six hours, Greenwood was to find himself wounded and taken prisoner by the Germans.

Major Dim Robbins (his name was Derek, but everyone knew him as Dim after his initials, D.I.M.) was a company commander with the 4th Wiltshires and he had spent a comfortable night in a château. He had a very good second-in-command called Chrisp, an Australian who was unfortunately killed a short while after the Seine crossing. Chrisp usually looked for somewhere nice and comfortable for 'C' Company's HQ.

On this occasion he had chosen a small château. Chrisp had informed the lady owner that his major always insisted on a good bed, with the best clean sheets. Robbins had never said any such thing and indeed felt rather embarrassed to be in such grand surroundings whilst he was so filthy from all the travelling. He thought he would sleep as he normally did, on the floor with just a blanket. Nevertheless, he succumbed to the heady pleasure of being between sheets again and spent a very pleasant night in the bed, his first since arriving in France.

At around 0600 hours on 25 August, Lieutenant-Colonel Tom Evill, the commander of the 43rd Division's engineers, arrived at the bridging site in Pacy. Throughout the previous night, engineers had been working feverishly to have the bridge ready for 0700 hours. Evill now found that events there had met a snag. The large gap in the demolished bridge was about forty feet (12m) wide and this gap was at that moment being closed with a length of Bailey, but the second span of the old bridge had been discovered to be cracked and suspect. From the look of it, it was unlikely that the damaged masonry would be able to stand up to the heavy pounding it would receive when tanks came to cross. Thus, although it would inevitably mean delays, Evill decided to play safe and extend the Bailey by a further thirty feet to take the strain off the second span. Nevertheless, there was some consolation to be had in the fact that the first part of the new construction would be strong enough for light reconnaissance jeeps and carriers to use. They, at least, would be able to cross on time and press on to the Seine on schedule.

At 0700 hours, the first of the armoured cars of the 43rd Reconnaissance Regiment slowly crossed over the new Bailey and negotiated the American diversion around the railway lines. Gathering speed, they climbed the hill out of the town and headed east for Vernon. Close behind them came an assortment of light vehicles belonging to the various survey parties, all anxious to get to the Seine as soon as possible so as to allow the maximum time to prepare for the crossing planned for later that evening.

The last eight miles (12km) to Vernon were covered at breakneck speed. Once the leading vehicles had quit Pacy, they headed out across the flat plateau towards the great river.

It was an exhilarating ride. Beneath a brilliant early morning sun which was already beginning to warm the clear air, the spearhead of the British army tore along the dusty road. Miles ahead of any other troops, this small column keenly felt their role as liberators.

Among the leading cars was Thomas with his ADC, Pat Spencer Moore. 'One of the most exciting trips I have ever had in my life,' recalls Spencer Moore. 'It was a marvellous summer's morning, and we were swanning through the countryside of France; the horrors of Normandy were all left far behind. It was a wonderful feeling.'

Midway between Pacy and the river the advance slowed almost to a halt. The road and nearby fields were a sea of craters. The group had reached La Huenière and the spot where the American 5th Armored Division had run into an ambush just five days before; 1,000lb bombs from the P47 Thunderbolts had pockmarked the area all around. Cynics among the British claimed that the devastation was a result of an American raid on the Seine bridges.

Contact was soon made with some American troops and Thomas was told that the bulk of the US forces had been withdrawn from the area, leaving patrols in Vernon until the British arrived to take over. They also explained that there had been three days of heavy fighting, just north of the Pacy-Vernon road, against enemy rearguards who were using their infantry and tanks to good effect in the close countryside. No guarantee could be given that this area was completely free of Germans. Until the situation was made clear, this left flank could not be considered safe.

In fact, this likelihood had already been envisaged, for Thomas had earmarked a squadron of the reconnaissance regiment, together with tanks of the 15th/19th King's Royal Hussars, to protect this northern area between the River Eure and the Seine.

A few miles further on, the road started to drop steeply as it began its winding descent into Vernon. The leading jeeps rounded a hairpin bend and suddenly there before them lay the town, with the Seine beyond.

The final approach into Vernon passed through the Forest of Bizy. Shielded by the trees, it was possible for the jeeps and carriers of the advance parties to slip into the town quietly, unnoticed by the local populace. So much so that the French civilians did not at first realise that the British had arrived, until they found the strange new vehicles parked on their doorsteps.

Thomas was one of the first to arrive in the town. He made straight for the river to look at the crossing sites that he had selected from the aerial photograph. He did not like what he saw. Across the wide river, the white chalk cliffs opposite dominated the waterfront; the crossing places were completely overlooked. It would take a prodigious amount of smoke to screen the assault from the enemy.

Closer at hand, there were more problems. The river bank was steep and muddy; it would be a struggle to get the DUKWs launched. Ramps would have to be bulldozed before the attack could even start. The resulting noise would almost certainly alert the Germans. Thomas urgently needed more local information about the river and its far bank. The general left the waterfront to look for the local FFI representatives.

As soon as they had arrived in Vernon, the reconnaissance parties had cautiously made their way down to the river. Thomas had felt that it was essential that the enemy be kept from learning that the British had arrived in the town, lest they realise that an assault was being mounted, and so he had ordered that anyone who approached the river and was likely to be seen should wear an American uniform, complete with helmet. Dressed in this foreign garb, the various survey teams representing all the arms of the division crept stealthily over walls and through gardens towards the water. Each of these groups began straining to obtain a complete picture of the riverbanks for its own special needs: the assaulting infantry commanders anxious to see the crossing sites and their objectives opposite, the engineers to view the landing places of the new bridges and the tank and artillery commanders to pinpoint likely targets.

All this activity attracted the attention of the local population. Word was out that the town had been properly liberated at last. Crowds began to gather around the British troops as they tried to move inconspicuously among the buildings near the waterfront. It all became quite embarrassing and potentially dangerous for the reconnaissance teams to be followed by so many civilians. Everyone wanted to help, each local claiming an intimate knowledge of the far bank.

Major Michael Concannon was the second in command of the 94th Field Regiment Royal Artillery and had arrived in the town with the leading parties to survey the sites for his regiment's guns. He remembers the local FFI men:

The resistance movement was very strong in Vernon, and we were approached by all kinds of people. We didn't know whether they were 'pukka' chaps or not. They wanted us to co-operate with them immediately. They all seemed to know where there was a German HQ, or a bunch of the enemy hiding out. We of course were anxious to get the attack started, and they couldn't understand why we, the liberators, had suddenly arrived and were not co-operating with them. We had to try to explain that we had come to Vernon to do a specific operation, and not to dash here and there after two or three Germans; we were after the whole lot. I think we may have annoyed some of them, but we had to be firm. Eventually they came to accept this.

Meanwhile, the divisional commander had found the FFI leaders he was looking for. The resistance men were in possession of the Château de Bizy, a grand eighteenth-century mansion set in ornamental parks overlooking the town.

The information they gave Thomas was encouraging. The major fears he had had about the sites chosen for the crossings appeared to have been unfounded. The landing point on the left flank for the 4th Somersets was indeed an island, but the cut separating it from the mainland was dry and passable. On the right above the blown road bridge, the 5th Wiltshires' crossing place was to pass over some weed-covered shallows. The local inhabitants insisted that the passage of any boats would not be hindered by these submerged islands. There was, they assured Thomas, sufficient depth of water. This was good news and the attack could go ahead as planned.

The information given by the locals concerning both sites was, however, quite wrong and, because of it, the whole operation would totter on the brink of disaster later that night.

By 1015 hours that morning, the bridge at Pacy was declared open. The whole of the Assault Group could now move on the Seine: DUKWs, lorries, jeeps, carriers, armoured cars and tanks all began their race to the river.

The normal instructions, insisting on set speeds and distances between vehicles moving in convoy, were ignored. Drivers were told to drive as close as they could get to each other, not at the regulation speed of 15mph, but flat out. In this way, in the four hours allocated to this first group, all of the 1,600 vehicles passed through the American checkpoint across the US lines of communication without any trouble.

Leading the Assault Group were the 4th Wiltshires. When the convoy reached the point in the route where the road began to drop down into Vernon, the 4th Wiltshires pushed on into the town, whilst the others pulled off the road into fields on either side.

The Wiltshire battalion was to take control of the town in order to provide a secure base from which the attack across the river could be launched. Locations in Vernon for each of the battalion's companies had been selected previously from the air photograph. These had recently been confirmed by ground reconnaissance and so the infantry were able to move straight into position, establishing themselves just back from the waterfront with a commanding view of the crossing sites. Observation posts were quickly set up and the enemy's movements monitored. There was little to be seen; the Germans on the opposite bank remained oblivious to the fact that a British division was concentrating just a short distance away.

Once the 4th Wiltshires had taken up their positions, still more parties came forward to do their own reconnaissance. Lieutenant-Colonel Lloyd,

Commander 7th Army Troops Royal Engineers, led a small party of men and vehicles, the latter consisting of his car, a jeep, a wireless truck and two dispatch riders, down into the town. Following the route he had memorised from the aerial photograph, his group moved towards the centre of Vernon near to the railway goods yard, where they set up their headquarters.

As an engineer, Lloyd was interested to find a trainload of bridging equipment in one of the sidings. A railwayman told him that it was German and its counterpart was across the other side of the river in Vernonnet. The Germans had intended to construct a pontoon bridge across the Seine, building out from each bank, but the whole project had been sabotaged when the French train mysteriously broke down soon after being ordered to move.

Lloyd's engineers were to build the first Bailey across the river after the completion of the light Class 9 folding boat bridge. The spot earmarked for the light bridge was about eighty yards (73m) upstream of the demolished road bridge, and just below this old bridge was the proposed site for Lloyd's Bailey. This latter bridge was the most important part of the whole operation, since, once opened, it would serve to rush tanks into the lodgement area against any possible German counter-attack. Then finally, when the bridgehead was secure, the Bailey bridge would carry over the Seine the whole of XXX Corps on their drive towards Belgium.

Lloyd needed to have a good look at the area just below the old Pont de Vernon that was to be his bridging site. The aerial photograph had left him in some doubt as to the possibility of fitting his bridge in the gap left between the old stone bridge and a small rocky island downstream. Scaling from the picture, he had estimated that there were twenty-one yards between the piers of the demolished structure and the island. As the pontoons used in the Bailey were twenty yards long, he reasoned that the alignment of his bridge might cause him some problems. He set off on foot to investigate.

Passing down a tree-lined street, he came to a large stone tower standing beside the town's fire station. The massive keep was all that remained of the twelfth-century castle built by Henry I. This 'Tour des Archives' now provided an excellent platform from which to survey the surrounding area.

On the roof was a hut with windows all round. Inside Lloyd found an American artillery officer engaged in the direction of some guns way back in the rear. The US officer was bringing down fire on enemy targets across the river that had been pinpointed by an enthusiastic Frenchman who had recently returned from Vernonnet. Whilst Lloyd watched through his field glasses, the shellfire flushed out a party of Germans from the house, much to the delight of the Frenchman who bobbed up and down with glee at each salvo. The British officer began to get a little worried at the antics of this

Gallic spectator, silhouetted as he was against the glass windows at the back of the hut. Lloyd found some board and covered up the rear windows, and was then able to concentrate on the site of the proposed bridge without further distraction.

He was not pleased with what he saw; the small island was very close to the old bridge and appeared to be composed of large rocks. He was sure that he would have to blast the end off it in order to fit his bridge in the gap. His attention then shifted to the river. The level was much lower than he had imagined. On the opposite side the bank was high, with a concrete retaining wall. This difference in height between the shore and what was to be the level of the first pontoon on the water might well produce an unacceptable slope; the top of the wall would have to be demolished. The near bank was not visible from the top of the tower because of the houses bordering the river. That too might pose further problems. All in all, the job of constructing this first Bailey was beginning to look as though it would be awkward and time-consuming.

Leaving the lofty tower, Lloyd cautiously made his way down to the river. Running parallel to the Seine was a road. At the junction of this road and the main thoroughfare feeding the old bridge were two large red-brick buildings, one on either side of the road. They had been spared the pattern bombing that had wrought such damage along the river-front. Lloyd entered the left-hand building and went upstairs.

From a window overlooking the Seine, the sapper officer had a good view of the bridging site. Although the river-front was high above the water, it might, he thought, be possible to bulldoze a gentle slope down to the new bridge. The only real problem here was the absence of a flat, or gently sloping, stretch of ground on which to build the landing bay prior to launching. The site looked difficult, but not impossible.

As the day wore on, the number of reconnaissance and survey parties wishing to see the river and its environs grew considerably. Strict orders were in force that anyone approaching the waterfront should take great care. The enemy still appeared to have no suspicion that an assault was likely and could be seen moving about on the far hillside quite openly. Thomas was keen to keep it that way. The 4th Wiltshires were now in total possession of the waterfront area and were controlling all movement down to the river, but the difficulties seemed to increase with the arrival of each new survey group, as their regimental historian explains:

We had found the atmosphere unreal enough, but it was harder for the new arrivals to realise that the whole position was overlooked by the enemy, and in our new capacity as traffic police we sweated blood in the afternoon sun, persuading men and vehicles to hide themselves away and not join the inhabitants in a liberation promenade. Now commanders of every rank and every arm crowded into our observation posts, and it took all our tact and persuasion to prevent their drawing expected fierce enemy reaction.

By mid-afternoon the preparations for the assault were well under way. To the north of the town, the broad Avenue des Capucins led down to the river. Lining each side of the wide thoroughfare was a double line of trees, the ample foliage of these trees joining at the top to form two long, green tunnels. In the shadows beneath, rows of DUKWs began to assemble for the crossing. Shielded from the view opposite, they were able to approach undetected almost to the river itself.

Along the routes into the centre of the town and in the streets a short way back from the river, parties of soldiers were busy signposting directions for the arriving troops. Everywhere there was furious activity: assembly areas and forming-up places were marked ready for the attacking infantry, stormboats were offloaded from RASC lorries, low loaders carrying bulldozers ground slowly through the narrow streets and, at every turning, fascinated French civilians watched each movement. They stood in small groups discussing what was going on and offering the benefit of their local knowledge. They all seemed to be dressed in their Sunday best clothes, the girls in pretty summer frocks. Again, the 4th Wiltshires' historian describes the scene: 'No work of any kind was being done; everybody was on the streets asking questions, accepting cigarettes, and giving advice with charming lavishness.'

The 8th Battalion Middlesex Regiment was the division's machine-gun battalion. It contained the heavy Vickers machine-guns and the large 4.2in mortars. Companies of these specialists were normally assigned to the three brigades during any attack. Two companies of the battalion had travelled forward with the Assault Group and had established themselves in buildings and gardens on either side of the old bridge. They were there to support the crossing and their three observation posts had already located enemy strongpoints.

More support for the attack, in the shape of Cromwell tanks from the 15th/19th King's Royal Hussars, arrived at the waterfront late in the afternoon. From their holding places just short of the town, two troops of tanks moved down the hill into Vernon. The Cromwells nosed carefully into positions selected for them during an earlier reconnaissance. Using the cover of buildings and manoeuvring gently down the narrow side streets, they were able to drive to within sixty yards of the river, all the while remaining unseen by the enemy opposite. The tank's 75mm guns were there to provide support to the assault, being able to give observed fire as directed by the infantry. This action at Vernon was to be the first battle fought by the regiment since its recent arrival in France.

Other heavy fire to support the attack was available from the artillery of the 94th Field Regiment. Their 25-pounder field guns were already in position in the Forest of Bizy. They were the only artillery included in the Assault Group; the remainder of the division's field guns and a regiment of medium artillery (5.5in) were due to arrive later in the evening with the Group 2 vehicles.

Slowly, and almost silently, Vernon was beginning to fill with the vast array of weapons and equipment of an assault division. The attack was still on schedule for 1900 hours (H-Hour); this time was considered to be the latest possible, as there was no moon that night. At 1800 hours, the commander of 129 Brigade, Brigadier Mole, called an 'orders group' to co-ordinate the final plan for the attack. Commanders from the four infantry battalions, the Royal Engineers and the Royal Artillery, as well as the divisional commander, were present.

Lieutenant-Colonel Tom Evill of the Divisional Engineers reported on his reconnaissance of the river. The site for his Class 9 folding boat bridge was confirmed and it was agreed that building would start as soon as the first infantry companies were across and were established. There did, however, appear to be a major problem in using DUKWs to carry the assaulting troops across: there were no suitable sites. The river banks were too steep to allow these long, low amphibious lorries to be driven into the water. To provide access ramps would involve more work than had been anticipated. It was recommended that stormboats be used during the initial phase, with ramps being bulldozed to take the DUKWs as soon as the first companies were over and dug in.

Unfortunately, the results of both the engineers' and the infantry's reconnaissances had not been fully co-ordinated and the decision to use stormboats came as a complete shock to the infantry commanders. They had never used the boats before and now had precious little time left to familiarise themselves with their operation. The 5th Wiltshires, in particular, were to suffer tragic consequences because of this. The remainder of the provisional plan was confirmed, with H-Hour set for 1900 hours.

Brigadier Mole then went on to outline the fire plan for the attack in detail. The artillery barrage was to open at H-Hour minus 15 minutes (1845). This would be supported by tank guns, machine guns and 4.2in mortars, concentrating on known and suspected enemy positions. At H-Hour, the artillery and mortars would switch to smoke. After a pause to allow the smoke-screen to build up, the infantry would begin the crossing; 5th Wiltshires on the right above the old road bridge, the 4th Somersets below, on the left.

When the 'O' group had finished, the two assault battalion commanders, Lieutenant-Colonel Bill Roberts of the 5th Wiltshires and Lieutenant-Colonel Lipscombe of the 4th Somerset Light Infantry, were left with little time to brief their men on the use of the stormboats. These long plywood boats were powered by Evinrude outboard motors and were able to carry about half a platoon, around eighteen men. Out of the water, they were extremely heavy and cumbersome to manoeuvre. It needed thirty-six men to carry one and, for those unused to doing so, a hundred yards was all that could be managed before exhaustion took over.

There was no way that the assaulting infantry would have the strength to carry their own boats down to the river, so carrying parties had to be found from elsewhere. As the precious minutes ticked away, men from the 4th Wiltshires were ordered to deal with the heavy task. To make matters worse, the stormboats had been offloaded earlier in the afternoon quite a distance from the river, as at the time there had been no intention of using them for the assault. It was going to be a struggle to get them into the water on schedule.

The last-minute decision to use stormboats was undoubtedly a problem for the infantry, but there was, nevertheless, one heartening factor: the boats were to be piloted by 583 Field Company from Fayle's 15th (Kent) GHQ Troops Royal Engineers, who were the army's foremost experts on boat handling. Fayle's unit had been selected to build a Class 70 bridge later in the operation (this had by then been altered to a Class 40 Bailey) and he had fortunately allocated 583 Field Company to the Assault Group for boating and rafting duties during the initial crossings.

A little way back from the river, hiding behind a hedge, was another group of Royal Engineers. Sergeant Pat Tucker was standing with his platoon beside their two bulldozers. Their work on the folding boat bridge would not start until much later and they were idling their time waiting for the attack to begin, when an official war photographer approached a section of the platoon. Tucker remembers the incident:

He wanted some action shots and as we had nothing better to do, we were happy to oblige. He asked us to get in battle formation with guns ready, and walk towards the camera. To do this we were actually walking away from the enemy when he took some shots. I heard later that one picture was published as 'Troops going into action at the Seine'.

With just thirty minutes to go before the start of the barrage, more support arrived to help the division. The 121 Medium Regiment Royal Artillery had led the Group 2 convoy and had reached the hillside overlooking Vernon. They immediately set about making their guns ready for action.

The regiment's passage through the American checkpoint in the second of the four-hour periods allocated to the division passed without a hitch. There would now be two regiments of artillery supporting the attack – still far short of what the infantry were used to. In fact, the division had never gone into action before with so few guns behind it and there was still to be another two hours before the other two field regiments had their guns in position.

Although Group 2 and its vehicles were now concentrating between Pacy and Vernon, they were not complete. The last three serials of the group, including 440 lorries with engineers and bridging equipment on board, were unable to pass the American checkpoint before the end of the allotted period at 1800 hours. The Americans were playing it strictly by the book. The route east was closed to British traffic; the engineers would have to wait.

By 1830 hours, the two assaulting battalions and the follow-up battalion, the 1st Worcestershires, had been fed and moved into the town. They were lined up behind the buildings along the waterfront, waiting for the artillery barrage to open. Preparations were complete; the division was ready to attack.

Situation at 1845 hours Friday 25 August
Both banks of the River Seine at Vernon were devoid of troops. Whilst the British 43rd Division remained hidden amongst the buildings of the town, poised to burst from cover and assault the river, the German Battle Group Meyer, opposite the 5th Wiltshires, was still oblivious to the impending attack. Surprise was to be complete.

The Wessex Division was as ready as it would ever be, but there still remained some niggling doubts: Could the 4th Somerset Light Infantry get across the cut separating its landing place from the mainland? Would the submerged islands in front of the 5th Wiltshires be deep enough to allow the stormboats to pass over? Would the lack of co-ordination between the infantry and engineers' reconnaissances of the crossing places be critical?

Chapter 8

The Assault

At 1845 hours, the first crash of guns sent the population of Vernon hurrying for cover. The liberation promenade of pretty girls in their summer frocks and men in their Sunday-best suits vanished in seconds as the shells whined low overhead towards the other side of the river. Soon the artillery guns back in the Forest of Bizy were joined by the tanks and mortars along the river-front in laying down a barrage of high explosives on to the white chalk cliffs opposite.

Fifteen minutes later the guns and mortars switched to smoke and mushroom-like puffs of white cloud slowly billowed up between the trees, gradually blotting out the hillside. Slowly, the other side of the river began to disappear from the view of the men crouched behind walls in the orchards along the Vernon side of the river bank. In reply, from out of this protective mist, came the familiar rattle of Spandau machine-gun fire; the enemy were waiting.

The muddy bank on the far shore led on to a strip of grassy meadow, edged by a road. Dotted along this road were a few houses and, behind these, a railway line running along the river valley. Rising precipitously behind the railway was a 300ft (91m) escarpment which stretched far to the right towards Giverny; the left-hand side dipped down into the village of Vernonnet. Superimposed on this feature, dominating the scene completely, was Battle Group Meyer. The enemy overlooked every movement on the Vernon side. A less inviting place to force a crossing would be difficult to imagine; everything seemed to favour the defenders.

'A' Company from the 5th Wiltshires had been selected to lead the right-hand assault. The company commander was 30-year-old Major James Fraser Milne. From the cover of the stone wall, Milne watched the bombardment impassively. His orders were simple: cross the river and hold the right flank against any enemy interference with the bridging site.

Only nineteen days before, Milne had been captured and had subsequently escaped during an attack on Mont Pinçon. He had been delayed in going forward with the leading waves by two reticent members of his company. When he finally moved up to join his men, he had walked

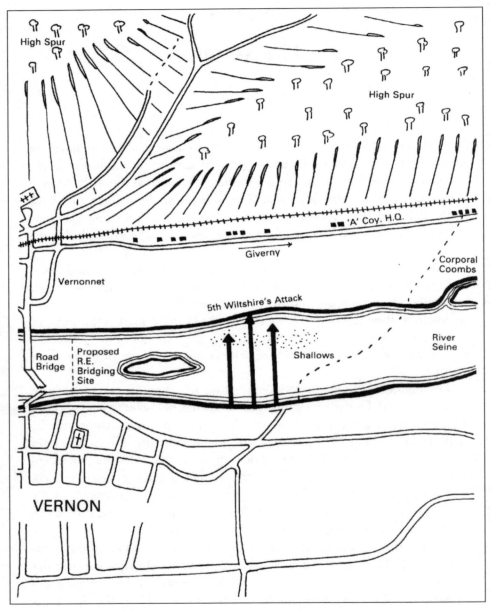

Map 4. Right-hand assault by 5th Wiltshires.

straight into a German slit trench and was taken prisoner. Later that day, whilst being moved back down the hill, he and his captors had been subjected to a heavy artillery barrage that knocked him to the ground. Milne feigned serious injury and was on the point of being shot when another fall of shells winded his would-be executioner. In the confusion, he had made good his escape. Within just a few more hours that night, he would once again be a captive of the German army.

Once the smoke-screen had completely obscured the far bank, the carrying parties started to bring the stormboats across the open ground to the water's edge. By that time they should have all been ready, just out of sight, near to the river. However, some were still a good way back in the town waiting for men to move them. It took about thirty-six troops to move one stormboat and there were sixteen to be carried forward for the two separate assaults, eight on each battalion front; a total of nearly six hundred men was needed to shift them. Such numbers of men were not readily available. Indeed, to provide that many troops would involve almost the whole of the 4th Wiltshires battalion and their main task was the defence of the town. Carrying parties were hurriedly made up from anyone who could be found. In consequence, the stormboats arrived at the river piecemeal.

It was an incredibly awkward job to manhandle the ungainly craft across the grassy area bordering the Seine; the infantry had no idea of how to move them properly. It proved another difficult and painfully slow task to get them down the steep bank and into the river. By the time the assault should have been under way, only two of the eight stormboats allocated to the 5th Wiltshires were in the water.

Into those two boats Lieutenant Selby and his No 8 Platoon began to embark. The lack of boats in the water meant that the assault could not go across in one wave as planned, but as and when each boat was ready. The steep banks made it difficult for the heavily laden infantry to climb into the boats. Engineers with long boathooks held the flat-bottomed vessels close against the shore, but they still rocked violently as each man stepped aboard. Then the craft pushed off and their engines were started.

Watching from the shore and recording the moment for posterity were two official war photographers. They took many still pictures and cine film of the two boats slipping out into the smoke-covered river before the tiny craft were finally swallowed up by the patchy fog and disappeared from sight. Those pictures were to become a final epitaph for most of the thirty-odd men from No 8 Platoon. Within the next few minutes, twenty-four of them were dead.

Everything seemed to be going well until, with about thirty yards to go, both boats grounded on a mudbank and came to an abrupt halt. The Wiltshires had stalled on the submerged island that the locals had assured Thomas was deep enough underwater to allow free passage. As chance would have it, the smoke-screen at that moment began to disperse. The German response to the attempted crossing was both immediate and savage. Machine-gun fire raked the small boats. Lieutenant Selby's craft, caught in a hail of bullets, capsized and threw all his section into the water; there were no survivors. The second boat was riddled with holes from stem to stern, but remained firmly held in the mud. Sergeant Mackrell, who headed this group, called for his men to swim to the far bank. He leapt into the river and, with the water all around him erupting from the enemy fire, made for the shore. On reaching the enemy side of the river, he found he was alone. The rest of his men had been shot or had drowned on the way: No 8 Platoon had completely disappeared.

Sergeant Mackrell crawled out of the water and up the muddy bank. He looked along the river expecting to see other boats coming across; there was none. Passing low above his head, the enemy fire continued to rake the ground all around him. Unable to raise his head because of this fire and convinced no one else was coming over, Mackrell slipped back into the water and swam back towards the boat.

Sheltering at the stern of the stormboat was the craft's pilot, a Royal Engineer officer called Bellamy. Inside was a wounded private. There was no other sign of life; the rest of the platoon had all been swept away downstream. Those who had escaped the enemy fire seemed to have been claimed by the river, their heavy packs dragging them under. The two survivors clambered aboard and attempted to start the engine, but this activity brought them further attention from the cliffs opposite. So, slipping back into the water, they swam round the wrecked boat and paddled it towards the shelter of the tree-covered island a little way downstream. Here they rested until they felt sufficiently strong to make it back to the friendly shore.

Meanwhile, other boats had arrived at the river's edge, and began the task of ferrying over the remainder of 'A' Company. A few had difficulty in starting their engines. This could only be done after all the troops were on board and the craft had pushed off; the Evinrude motors had no clutch, so the engines could not be running as the infantry embarked. These powerless stormboats drifted downstream in the current and ran aground. Others had their propellers fouled by weeds and remained stranded in mid-river, sometimes drifting out of the patchy smoke into bright sunlight, at the mercy of the German machine-guns.

The smoke-screen was becoming very sparse as the slight breeze began to carry it away. It was a formidable task for the artillery and mortars to keep the long stretch of river shrouded in its protective mist. Parts of the water inevitably emerged into full view of the opposite hills. Through these gaps, the clinically efficient enemy fire caused great damage, sinking boats and picking off the men struggling for their lives in the cold water. By good fortune, a large number of these men made it back to the near shore, where they dragged themselves, exhausted, up the steep banks and made for the shelter of the stone walls around the orchards near the river.

In one of those boats was Fred Greenwood, a signaller attached to the Wiltshires. He sat at the back of the stormboat with his no 18 radio set in front of him for protection. His craft had almost reached the centre of the river when the smoke cleared and they were spotted by an enemy machine-gun. Bullets began to smash into the plywood boat, hitting some of the men crouched in the front and piercing holes all along the waterline. The craft immediately started to take in water, much to the alarm of the overburdened troops. There were cries for the helmsman to head back for shore, for it very soon became clear that the boat would never make it to the far side. The engineer in charge of the craft quickly brought its bows around and went full speed for the near bank.

To Major Milne, waiting by the water's edge for his turn to cross, it appeared that this boat was refusing to go over. With pistol drawn, he ran along the bank, urging them back across the river. At this point the waterlogged boat foundered, tipping all its contents into the water. The dead and injured that could not be reached simply floated away downstream. Fred Greenwood managed to struggle ashore, wading through chest-deep water with his wireless above his head in an attempt to keep it dry. Once out of the river, he ran across the open ground and ducked behind a stone wall to escape the chaos on the river-front. He had had enough; it was time for a rest and a crafty cigarette.

Other boats on the river were having an equally hard time in getting across. The next stormboat contained Major Milne and the company HQ and his attempt suffered the same fate as previous ones. Once again, when the stormboat reached about half way, it was caught by enemy machine-guns and hit repeatedly. Within minutes the boat had sunk with dreadful casualties. Those who were able swam back to the near shore. The crossing was becoming a shambles.

There was one stormboat, however, that had a relatively easy crossing. This set off from the extreme right-hand end of the 5th Wiltshires' position. The furthest upstream of all the boats, it was away from the worst of the firing, and clear of the shallow mudbanks in mid-river. On board were Corporal Vic Coombs and his section.

Coombs was of the opinion that the stretch of water they were about to cross was deadly. There was virtually no smoke on that section of the river; the visibility was good and the hillside opposite dominated everything. The helmsman must have been of the same opinion, for he did not take a direct route over the water, but navigated a long detour upstream, away from all the chaos near to the island. Surprisingly, the crossing was uneventful and Coombs does not recall any shots being fired at them.

Once across, the corporal was faced with another hazardous task. His objective was a group of houses along the road beneath the escarpment, a few hundred yards away across open meadows. The intervening stretch of green fields was completely devoid of smoke and was bathed in evening sunshine. Between the river and the road there was not one single piece of cover. If they were spotted by the enemy on the hilltop, it was unlikely anyone would make it to the road alive.

Coombs gave his men one simple order: 'Heads down, and run like stink for the road.' They did so and reached their objective without any mishaps. The houses were clustered together between the road and the railway line and rising precipitously behind were the enemy-dominated high chalk cliffs. Once in the houses, Coombs and his men were out of sight of the German defenders on the hilltop, whose guns were trained out towards the wide river.

The Wiltshiremen immediately set about organising an all-round defensive position blocking the road, in order to protect the right-hand flank of the proposed initial bridgehead and allow the company to get established. Within a short while, things began to happen.

Along the road came a bicycle patrol; six whistling Germans on push bikes, seemingly oblivious to the dangers they faced. The British infantry let them ride right up to their lines before knocking them off their bikes and taking them prisoner. They had no idea that any hostile troops were over the river and were flabbergasted. A guarded room in one of the houses served as a prison. Then the Wessexmen settled down to await events.

Throughout the next hour shots could be heard coming from back along the road towards Vernonnet, although none was fired at Coombs and his men. All the action seemed to be taking place near the waterfront. A lone soldier came up from the river with the news that the platoon's officer, Lieutenant Drake, was dead, killed whilst trying to cross the open meadows between the river and the road. This was a blow to Vic Coombs, who was by now expecting to receive some orders. He was also a little surprised, because everything seemed so quiet around his area of the bridgehead. He was just about to send the man back to find an officer and get some orders, when the fellow spotted a German cyclist coming down the road from the direction of Giverny. Foolishly, the soldier opened fire with his Sten gun. He missed the German by miles and the startled cyclist turned quickly and cycled away. Coombs was furious; the enemy would now know they were across and he could soon expect a counter-attack to be launched against his small force.

Back across the river, the wet and weary signaller Fred Greenwood had finished his cigarette and was taking full advantage of his rest from the action on the river. He was trying to convince a fellow operator that there were plenty of others available to fight the war and that they should stay where they were for a while, when the colonel popped his head over the wall and told them that another boat was ready.

The boat that Lieutenant-Colonel Roberts had found was, in fact, the only one still surviving from the original eight; all the others had been sunk or damaged beyond further use. This solitary stormboat was manned by Lieutenant Bellamy, the Royal Engineer in charge of the boating platoon. After recovering from his ordeal in the water on the first waves of the assault, he was now back ferrying others across. Wearing only a duffle coat and a pair of socks, he continued to pilot his boat on a wide detour upstream, avoiding the worst of the gunfire and the submerged islands. On one trip, this longer journey across led to problems for a signals party he was carrying. The signalmen were paying out telephone cable as they went, and reached the end of the drum before they arrived on the other side. For a while at least, communications with the forward troops would have to rely on radio.

Fred Greenwood's second attempt at crossing was more successful, since the longer route upstream was relatively quiet. Unfortunately, in his hurry to get over, the helmsman misjudged his speed as he approached the bank and struck it with such force that the boat rebounded back into the river. By the time it was Greenwood's time to disembark, the boat had drifted away from the water's edge. Eager to get off the craft, he gave an almighty leap for the shore, but missed and landed back in the river. For the second time that evening, both he and his wireless were floating about in the Seine.

Greenwood's group of about fifteen men, together with an officer, assembled in a hollow by the side of the river before moving off towards their objective, a large white house about three hundred yards away across open fields. It was still light and, through the thin smoke-screen, they could hear the sound of small-arms fire all around them, although it was difficult to pinpoint where it came from. Moving from hollow to hollow, they made for the house by a circuitous route and arrived at what had already become the company headquarters without attracting any fire.

At the house was Major Milne with about fifteen men. His group had had another stormy crossing, having again been subjected to fierce enemy fire in mid-river and having lost a sergeant-major on the way. The house, a large barn-like structure, had not been in recent occupation. It had a few outbuildings, among which Milne set about organising a defensive position with the remains of his two surviving platoons. The approaches from the road and railway line were covered from slit trenches hastily dug in the garden. They would soon have to deal with the expected enemy reaction to their presence, probably from the direction of Giverny. Those of the enemy behind them in Vernonnet were less likely to venture out whilst the two simultaneous assaults were taking place, above and below the village. However, before any of the enemy could move against 'A' Company's HQ, they first had to get past Coombs and his section covering the road from the group of houses further up the valley.

By this time, Corporal Coombs and his men were feeling the effects of the first German probes along the road towards the landings. The enemy had gathered behind some trees about a hundred yards from the houses and began advancing along a ditch that ran alongside the road. They were met with a hail of rifle and Bren-gun fire from the house and fell back.

The next attempt came both along the road and railway track and was supported by a heavy machine-gun set back in the trees. This was a more determined effort and it took another furious exchange of fire before the enemy retired.

This small band of the 5th Wiltshires had only the ammunition that they had carried over the river with them; no other supplies had reached their positions. The two fierce attacks had been beaten off, but at the expense of a large amount of ammunition. It would not take long before they ran out altogether. In view of the fact that he had not been given any contrary orders, Coombs decided to fall back down the road a short distance and hole up in another house nearer company HQ.

Whilst the rest of his section dropped back, Coombs and a Bren gunner fought a rearguard action, firing from the tops of garden walls, gradually giving way until they reached the last of the group of houses. Here they met Major Milne, who had come up from his headquarters to see the situation in this outpost for himself. By this time, they were down to almost the last bullet and Milne agreed that without ammunition the situation would soon become critical. The major told Coombs to organise a withdrawal back down the valley to join up with the rest of the company.

Whilst this withdrawal was being organised, the enemy was becoming bolder. Coombs saw a large German creeping along the ditch by the side of the house, carrying a machine-gun. The enemy soldier then began to set it up right outside the house they were in, no more than ten yards away. Evidently the Germans thought that the British had all gone. It was an opportunity too good to miss. Coombs, completely out of ammunition, took a rifle, scrounged a bullet and shot the man dead. (He later regretted this action, for having been taken prisoner Coombs was forced to carry this very heavy German back to a field hospital.)

This action convinced the Germans that the Wiltshires were still prepared to continue the fight and their reaction was both fierce and noisy. Heavy machine-guns fired continually at the house and along the road. There was no longer any chance of escape for the British infantry cornered inside. It did not take long before all their ammunition was gone, and there was only one course of action left open to the trapped section. During a lull in the firing, a white towel tied to a rifle was held out. Corporal Vic Coombs and five men, all that remained, filed out of the house and into captivity.

At 'A' Company's HQ it was beginning to get dark and Major Milne was anxious to get in touch with battalion HQ. Signaller Greenwood's radio had twice been immersed in the water during the crossing and he found, not surprisingly, that it would not work. The radio would receive, but not transmit. All was not lost, however, for in the house was an observer from the Royal Artillery, together with his signaller. By chance, their set could send but not receive. Greenwood suggested that the two sets be combined, so that at least one group could contact the rear area and report on events. As the two radios used different frequencies, the gunner's transmit channel would have to be changed. This was no easy task, for tuning a wireless was an exact art and they were usually carefully set up before the start of an operation. Nevertheless, through skill, or perhaps just good luck, Greenwood eventually got through to battalion HQ, making the first radio link by the British army across the Seine.

By now, the enemy had moved down the valley and was clashing with the perimeter of the company's defences. This first attack was beaten off with some casualties. Before long the enemy tried again, a more concerted effort this time, supported by mortars. A message was sent back to the battalion, requesting artillery support. When it arrived, however, it fell more on the 5th Wiltshires than on the enemy, so close were the two sides together. It turned out to be too dangerous to be effective and was abandoned.

Every available weapon was called upon to lay down a curtain of fire against the enemy, but in the darkness they still managed to press forward almost to the HQ building itself, before they fell back in the face of such fire. The small stock of ammunition brought over the river by the company was

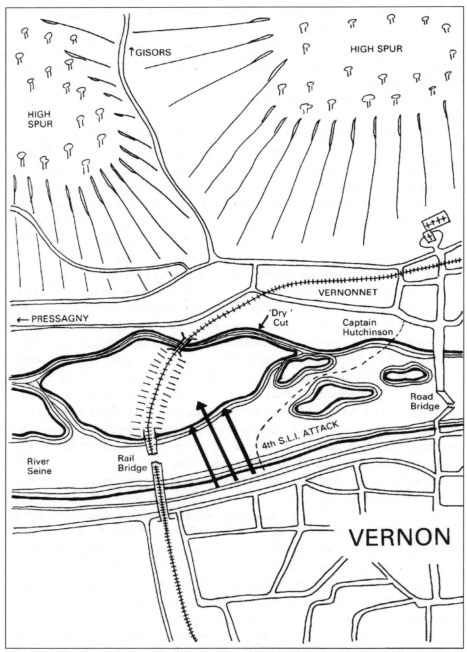

Map 5. Left–hand assault by the 4th Somerset Light Infantry.

being quickly depleted and no immediate replenishment seemed likely; the stormboats on the river were busy bringing troops across, not supplies. The follow-up company was not intended to move to 'A' Company's assistance, its objective being in the other direction towards Vernonnet and the site of the new bridge. For the moment at least, Major Milne and his men would have to deal with the counter-attack on their own.

Downstream of the demolished road bridge was the area that had been selected for the other half of this two-pronged attack across the River Seine. This left-hand assault was to be carried out initially by 'A' Company of the 4th Somerset Light Infantry.

The site chosen for the crossing was just upstream of the ruined railway bridge. As in the attempt by the 5th Wiltshires, eight stormboats had been allocated to the battalion, to be piloted by Royal Engineers. Carrying parties again found considerable difficulty in getting the heavy boats down into the river, but this time they had been dropped off the RASC lorries nearer to the Seine. In consequence, at H-Hour, most of the boats were in the water ready for the signal to go across.

The proposed landing site opposite was covered with a sprinkling of trees, which would give the infantry some shelter when they landed. There was more concealment available in the shape of the railway embankment that ran inland from the water's edge. Although the area was overlooked by another of the high chalk spurs that are so common along this stretch of the Seine, it did look a better proposition than that which confronted the Wiltshires.

In one of the first stormboats to attempt the crossing was Corporal Hitchcock. He remembers coming under fire, in mid-river, from an anti-aircraft gun firing small shells. One boat was immediately hit and sank near the shore; the others all made it safely across. Once on the far side, the troops leapt ashore and made for the cover of the railway embankment. Small enemy shells were bursting everywhere, probing through the thick smoke-screen. Those that burst in the tree-tops sent red-hot splinters of steel in all directions, giving the infantry added incentive to get below ground as quickly as possible. One green young private, newly arrived with the unit, was going into action for the first time. As he dug in next to Corporal Hitchcock, he talked nervously about a parcel he had just received from home. In describing the parcel's contents – a pair of socks, a woolly helmet and a chocolate cake – he must have straightened up, for he received a direct hit from one of the shells and died instantly. He had been with the company for such a short time that no one even knew his first name.

On the far side of the landing site was a cut formed by a small tributary; this was the cut that the Army Photographic Interpretation Section had decided was almost certainly dry and should be passable to infantry. To determine whether vehicles could be transported over by this route, Lance-Sergeant Rex Hunt, an engineer from the division's 260 Field Company, was sent across with the leading company to reconnoitre.

Hunt and his party came under accurate fire even before they embarked, from an unlocated machine-gun further upstream. The bullets were striking the ground all around them as they raced for cover. A few minutes later, when the smoke-screen had thickened, they made another attempt to get to the boat and were more successful. After an uneventful crossing, Hunt remembers landing on the other side of the river by a clump of fir trees near the old railway bridge. Together with an officer of the 4th Somersets, he then made his way across a patch of open ground towards the obstacle. Sniper fire caused them to take evasive action and race for the trees lining the cut. This small cut turned out in fact to be a deep watercourse, some sixty feet (18m) wide with steep muddy banks. It was clearly too wide to be bridged except by a length of Bailey and, as there were no approach roads to it, this was ruled out. Far from being passable, it was unlikely that anyone would ever get across to the mainland that way.

'A' Company had landed on what was virtually an island, but this was not immediately known to them. They continued to establish the bridgehead, with the troops straightaway digging slit trenches for protection. The stormboats returned to the near shore and began to ferry over the second company, 'C' Company, which was to pass through 'A' Company's positions and head inland.

Captain Hancock, from the 94th Field Regiment Royal Artillery, was the forward observation officer attached to the 4th Somersets. It was his job to co-ordinate the supporting artillery fire given to the infantry, from the field guns back in the Forest of Bizy. To help him do this, he needed to have with him radio equipment and other kit which was all rather bulky to carry. He had previously arranged to have all this kit taken over the river in a jeep, loaded onto a stormboat.

Under the cover of smoke, the precarious job of getting the jeep into the boat was accomplished without too much difficulty, but the problems came once the stormboat arrived on the far shore. The banks were covered in thick mud and were much too sticky for the jeep to traverse without bogging down. A ramp would have to be constructed. Some girders and a pile of logs were found and, with some ingenuity and a lot of effort, a runway was built. Carefully the jeep was manhandled ashore. Captain Hancock and his driver jumped in and sped off to join the forward troops. Unfortunately, they did not have far to travel, for the two companies over the river had discovered that the bridgehead consisted of an island. They controlled an area of only 150 by 100 yards (137 x 91m).

Attempts were made to get off the island. Some of 'A' Company tried to cross the muddy watercourse by following the railway embankment and attempting the short, exposed railway bridge to the mainland. As they crept along its side ledge, holding on to the parapet wall, they were spotted by some enemy infantry dug in nearby, who opened fire on them with rifles. With bullets striking the superstructure all around them, a few of the Somersets continued to the far side and took cover in the gardens alongside the water. The remainder fell back when the enemy fire was taken up by the machine-guns high up on the hill. A halt was called to this hazardous operation. The only way forward off the island was effectively barred. As it was by that time becoming dark, the only choice remaining was to dig in for the night.

Once it had become dark, the Germans began probing the Somersets' positions. Captain Hancock could hear their movements as they approached the island. Using his wireless, he passed a location back to the guns and, estimating the range by sound, brought down fire on the enemy, forcing them to retire. Each time they ventured too close to the bridgehead, the enemy were dealt with in this way and the rest of the night passed peacefully for 'A' and 'C' Companies.

In its original form, the operation called for an assault on two fronts: the 5th Wiltshires on the right, above the old road bridge, and the 4th Somersets below it on the left. The 1st Worcestershires were to follow the 5th Wiltshires over, pass through their positions and take over the centre of the bridgehead, with their perimeter well forward on the high spur behind Vernonnet.

When the artillery barrage opened, the Worcestershires were waiting in their vehicles for the order to move down to the river bank. After a while, it became evident that the first waves of the assault were not going according to plan. Reports began to filter back of the troubles being experienced by the Wiltshires. It would be a long time before any more troops could be put across on the right.

In the failing light, General Thomas met with the commander of 129 Brigade, Brigadier Mole, down by the water's edge, near the old bridge. With him was his ADC, Pat Spencer Moore, who remembers the scene:

I could see that Thomas was a little agitated, and caught snatches of his conversation with Brigadier Mole. He seemed to be trying to get Mole to move the 4th Somersets to a new site and prodded the map, saying, 'Have you tried to get in round there?' The plan was obviously going wrong.

What Thomas and Mole did decide was that the only crossing place still remaining that was untried was over the ruins of the old road bridge itself. Thomas ordered Mole to try to put the 1st Worcestershires over the stone bridge, straight into the village of Vernonnet.

The wrecked Pont de Vernon looked to be still passable to men on foot. The ruins left by the French resistance when they sabotaged the bridge a few days before had completed the destruction started by the US Air Force, with the first few broken spans having collapsed into a huge 'V' shape. The rest of the bridge was virtually intact.

As dusk was falling, the leading platoon of 'A' Company from the 1st Worcestershires made their way through the back streets of Vernon towards the broken bridge. It was an unenviable task that awaited them, for the Germans were almost certain to have the bridge covered. Just to the right was an area being cleared by the Royal Engineers in preparation for the construction of the first boat bridge. This activity was attracting a great deal of attention from mortar and machine-gun fire on the other side, making that part of the river a most inhospitable place. In return, the 1st Worcestershires' own mortars were lobbing bombs across the river to cover the attack.

The Vernon end of the road bridge was stuck high in the air, with its redundant traffic lights still attached, pointing aimlessly down the road. To get on to the bridge, each man in turn had to climb a ladder and, on reaching the top, was silhouetted against the sky.

Ken Lugg was a private in 'A' Company's leading platoon, which after the losses suffered in earlier fighting in Normandy numbered about twenty. They were led by Sergeant Jennings, a man well respected by his troops, who would willingly have followed him anywhere. Lugg was confident, if a little scared, as they approached the ladder and began to go over. It was here that a burst of machine-gun fire caught and killed one of the men as he reached the top, his body falling onto the bridge and down the steep slope to the water. The other men in turn quickly jumped from the ladder onto the ruins and slithered down the broken span to water level. The gap at the bottom was crossed using pieces of timber and then they began the steep climb up the next broken span to the undamaged section. This was a long flat stretch, with the houses of Vernonnet looking down onto the bridge.

Slowly Sergeant Jennings led his platoon along the roadway, with bullets ricocheting off the steelwork as the men inched their way forward. At the end of the bridge was a road block. Jennings went forward to inspect it but touched a trip-wire before he got there. There was an explosion and Jennings was badly wounded; several others were injured.

The noise seemed to draw even more fire, this time directed at the bridge exit from a large concrete pillbox-like structure, situated just to the right of the road about fifty yards (45m) from the bridge. This machine-gun had the platoon completely pinned down, and it was impossible to move forward. The platoon was ordered to pull back off the bridge to the safety of Vernon. There could be no crossing by this route until the offending machine-gun had been taken out.

Another attempt to cross the river had come to nothing; Thomas's troubles seemed to be increasing. It was by now quite dark and his plan was falling behind schedule.

Situation at 2259 Friday 25 August

Almost four hours after the first stormboat had taken to the water, the 43rd Division had only a handful of troops over the river onto the mainland the other side. Of those across, Major Milne's lone company of the 5th Wiltshires was gradually being whittled away by German troops trying to move down the valley to link up with Vernonnet. Half a mile away downstream, the two companies of the 4th Somerset Light Infantry were isolated on their island. In the centre of the action, the way across the ruined bridge was effectively barred. The operation was in danger of becoming a shambles.

Chapter 9

Consolidation

At around 2300 hours, General Thomas and Brigadier Mole met yet again to review the situation. The prospect they faced was a bleak one, for the whole assault had stalled and needed a rethink. Thomas immediately decided that changes had to be made to the original plan. He ordered Lieutenant-Colonel Lipscombe to land his next two companies of the 4th Somersets further upstream, nearer to Vernonnet and, whenever possible, his two stranded companies were to be re-embarked and follow them over. At daybreak, the 1st Worcestershires were to make another attempt to force the partly demolished road bridge, at whatever the cost. To help them, the 5th Wiltshires would put their next two companies over downstream of the beleaguered 'A' Company nearer the old bridge, then move towards Vernonnet and capture the far exit. Thomas now placed the clearing of the village of Vernonnet at the top of his priorities. He had to have the proposed bridging sites under his control as soon as possible. For a few more hours at least, the luckless remainder of the 5th Wiltshire's 'A' Company would have to hold off the enemy counter-attack as best they could.

At around the same time that Thomas was meeting with his brigadier, German reinforcements began to arrive in Vernonnet, entering the rear of the village from the direction of Gisors. They were infantry from I Battalion of the 148 Grenadier Regiment, part of the 49th German Infantry Division. They had orders to relieve Battle Group Meyer for one day and then withdraw to form the regimental reserve. They found, however, that far from relieving static positions along the Seine, they had walked straight into a battle that was in full swing. As they arrived in the village, they were immediately fed into the line by platoons to fill gaps in the defences.

The battalion had left Boulogne ten days previously, the infantry leading the way on push bikes. By the time they had arrived in the area, their numbers had been sadly depleted by punctures and other mishaps on the way. They had no artillery or other support from heavy weapons and were typical of the disorganised state of the German army in France at that time.

Each company in the battalion originally consisted of three light and one heavy platoons, but they had lost half their strength providing replacements

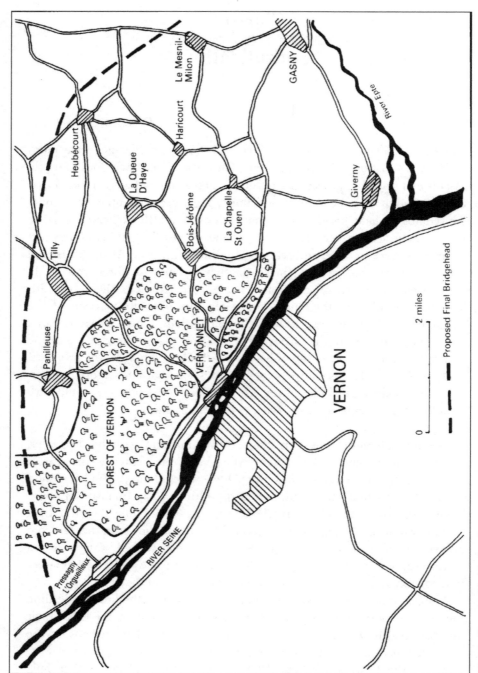

Map 6. Proposed bridgehead.

for the German 7th Army's losses in Normandy. Two months earlier, one light platoon had been disbanded. At the same time the mortars disappeared from the heavy platoon, along with the two heavy machine-guns allotted to the rifle platoons. In this way the 49th Division was gradually eroded of its fighting strength without ever coming into action, leaving a demoralised unit largely made up from press-ganged foreigners and Hitler Youth.

The arrival in Vernonnet of the 1/148 Grenadier Regiment came at a most opportune moment for the enemy. The Wessex Division's assault was by then well under way and there could no longer be any doubt that Vernonnet, with its road network, was its objective. These fresh troops stiffened the defences at a time when they were most needed. The village had been virtually devoid of any German presence for most of the preceding week. It was a cruel coincidence that brought this new enemy infantry there just when the British were contemplating its capture.

As a result of the losses suffered in the first waves of the assault, the 5th Wiltshires' stretch of the river had only one stormboat left in operation. Colonel Roberts was therefore forced to consider other means of getting his battalion safely over the Seine. The obvious choice was the DUKWs waiting a short distance away in the side streets of the town. However, everyone realised that they would be very difficult to launch down the steep banks and into the river. Ramps would be a solution to the launching problems, but the chaos along the waterfront had prevented the bulldozers from starting work.

Roberts urgently needed more infantry across the river as quickly as possible and so he gave orders for an attempt to be made to try to get DUKWs into the water. It was a failure: the first one grounded at the bottom of the bank; the second got stuck in mid-river and was shot up by the enemy. There was a pause whilst the 260 Field Company Royal Engineers came forward and built a ramp.

The site chosen for the slipway was well to the right of the 5th Wiltshires' positions on the near bank. An armoured bulldozer was allocated to the platoon involved, to clear the undergrowth and reduce the gradient down to the river. To cover the operation, the sappers were given the protection of a smoke-screen, laid and maintained by some mortars set back in the gardens along the riverside.

Sergeant Pat Tucker, in charge of the platoon, remembers making quite good progress until the smoke began to thin out and they were spotted from the opposite bank. The engineers were fired at by an anti-aircraft gun set high up on the clifftop. What made this particularly frightening was the fact that the enemy gun was firing tracer shells and the unfortunate engineers could actually see the projectiles snaking towards them. The only cover available to the party was the bulldozer itself, and it was an eerie sensation for them to shelter behind its thick blade as it was being spattered by the small enemy shells. Tucker called for more smoke, it being impossible to move without drawing enemy fire.

The smoke arrived, but continued to be rather patchy as it drifted about on the breeze.

Assistance was fortunately at hand from Corporal Phelps and his section, who were dug in at a short distance from the ramp. There to provide some local protection to the sappers, they began to sweep the area around the source of the tracer with Bren-gun fire. This return fire was taken up by one of the 15th/19th Hussars' tanks situated in a side street behind. The Cromwell sent several high-explosive shells screaming across the river to successfully silence the troublesome enemy gun.

In the gathering darkness, work managed to continue intermittently until the ramp was finished and the DUKWs were able to take to the water. Again it was not a great success, for although several were launched, most ran into problems. The mudflats in mid-stream still gave trouble to the few that were in use, and eventually one craft grounded at the foot of the ramp, putting it out of action completely.

By the time it was dark, the Wiltshires were still bedevilled by their transport problems. Only one DUKW was in use on the river and one surviving stormboat. These two craft were the only means of transport across this section of the Seine. Alone, they had to cope with ferrying the whole of the follow-up companies over into the bridgehead.

The battalion's foothold on the far shore was a precarious one. Roberts was anxious to get his second company across to prevent any of the enemy moving up the river valley from Vernonnet against his 'A' Company, which was already being pressed from the other direction. It took several hours to ferry the next company, 'C' Company, over and organise the men into an effective unit. They then held the centre of the Wiltshires' bridgehead whilst 'D' Company began its slow passage across, ready to move against Vernonnet. At a time when there was desperate need to quickly reinforce and expand the lodgement area, the follow-up troops were being introduced into the action at a rate solely dependent on the turn-around time of the two craft available. It was a most frustrating time for the battalion, made more so by the knowledge that their first company over was being sorely pressed by a determined attack.

Several hundred yards to the right of the positions that 'C' Company had taken up on its arrival on the far shore lay the house that contained 'A'

Company's HQ. This large white house was now under attack from the enemy, who were advancing down the road and railway track. Twice the German attacks had been broken up by a great concentration of fire from the rifles and Bren guns of the British infantry. Then came a third attempt, which managed to get even closer to the Wiltshires' perimeter, before the enemy were finally repulsed by the sheer volume of fire aimed at them. It had been a very close thing: the next attack might well be successful, for the continual firing had depleted the company's ammunition stocks. With no resupply from across the river, this small band of about twenty men had only a handful of rounds between them. Faced by what was believed to be an attack of at least company strength, the time had come for a limited withdrawal to link up with the rest of the battalion. The men in the slit trenches realised this. In ones and twos, they crept out from their cover and slipped quietly away in the darkness towards the river.

Inside the house, Greenwood and the other signallers knew nothing of this retreat, but from the commotion outside Greenwood realised that the enemy were pressing the defences hard. During the last attack, he had expected that at any moment Germans would burst through the door with bayonets raised. It was evident to him that the end was near, so he hid the radio's codes and grabbed a rifle ready to defend himself. When he checked the other rooms he was shocked to find how few of the company remained: just Major Milne and five other ranks.

Outside the Germans were raking the headquarters with machine-gun fire and illuminating the area with Very lights. They had seen the movements around the HQ and realised that the Wiltshires were trying to slip away. Escape now seemed impossible.

Major Milne was determined to make a last stand. He ordered the men to pile their radios and packs across a large hole that had been blown in the front of the house. Behind this, the men all lay with their weapons pointing down the road towards the enemy, waiting for the next attack. As it developed, the small group held their fire, conserving, for as long as possible, their last few precious bullets.

The shooting stopped and there followed a brief silence as the enemy waited to see if fire was returned. When none came, they assumed the Wiltshires had all fled and began to move along the road towards the house. The sound of their boots on the road seemed to fill the night air. Then the noise became muffled as the enemy soldiers stepped onto the grass and approached the buildings. Fred Greenwood was amazed by the stupidity of the enemy, who walked quite openly up to the house. All the while those inside lay motionless, watching until, at almost point-blank range, they opened fire.

Four rifles, a Sten and Major Milne's pistol wreaked havoc with the surprised Germans. Their officer, an immensely tall man, fell dead just feet away from the barricade; the others turned and fled. For the second time that night, this band of the enemy had made the mistake of thinking that the British had pulled out because there was no return of fire. As was to be expected, they were furious. All hell then broke loose on the Wiltshiremen. Everything the enemy could muster was aimed at the house: machine-gun fire, small arms fire, mortar bombs and grenades poured into the building. Everyone inside was hit: Greenwood in the face, Milne in the hand, one signaller had a bullet pass through the underside of his arm without being aware of it until the fighting was over, and another private, hit in the neck, fell across Major Milne, covering him with blood.

Now completely out of ammunition, there was little these men could do but crouch low and wait for the end. The next lull in the firing enabled them to call a halt to this one-sided battle. Greenwood and one of the other signallers moved to the back of the house with a view to making a run for it, but as they were arguing as to who should go first, events overtook them with the arrival of German soldiers at the front of the house, calling 'Tommy' and 'Kamerad'. Their fighting war had come to an end.

'A' Company's resistance was over. Their spirited defence of the bridgehead's right flank, without any support or resupply, had held out long enough for the rest of the battalion to get across the river and establish itself. Fred Greenwood later remarked that he had felt they were expendable. He was probably right, for although the company frequently called for reinforcements and more ammunition, none ever arrived. This was partly because of the confusion at the crossing sites, with the lack of ferries, and partly due to the need to have more troops further down the river valley, nearer Vernonnet. The left flank of the Wiltshires' lodgement had to be made secure before any assistance could be sent to the hard-pressed 'A' Company, for the capture of Vernonnet was the key to the success of the whole operation. Early possession of the village would enable work to start on the building of the first of the proposed bridges by the Royal Engineers. The far exit for this bridge was expected to be about ninety yards (82m) upstream of the old road bridge, just on the edge of Vernonnet. The far side of the river had to be made secure before bridging operations could begin. Therefore, it was towards this village that 'D' Company headed, after their arrival on the enemy side of the river.

In the middle of the night, Roberts landed with his advance battalion HQ among the positions held by 'C' Company. He immediately led a party of men down the road towards the hard-pressed 'A' Company, but was too late;

he arrived in the area near the house just at the time Milne's group was suffering its last attack. In the darkness, Roberts was unable to tell what was happening and so lay up among a group of trees. It was not long before he realised the outcome of this final skirmish and with it the sorry fate of 'A' Company.

By this time, another ramp had been bulldozed and there were more DUKWs in use on the river. The last of the battalion's companies, 'B' Company, now crossed and was given the task of protecting the right flank against the enemy moving down the valley. It did not prove to be necessary, for having overrun 'A' Company, the Germans did not push on down the road with much vigour. Evidently they did not welcome further close-quarters fighting in the dark, preferring to let the opposition to the landings come from the machine-guns in their well-protected posts up on the high ground. So, with the road along the valley once again blocked to the enemy, it was to this high ground that 'C' Company looked to extend the centre of the lodgement area.

Lieutenant Holly was the sole officer of an under-strength 'C' Company. In pitch darkness he led his men over the road and railway line towards the steep cliffs. This high escarpment, that so dominated the battalion's bridgehead, still bristled with machine-guns. The objective was for this company to gain the top of the feature and hold until help arrived; then to sweep along its length to clear the enemy from their dug-in positions overlooking Vernon and the bridging sites.

The climb up the chalky rock face was made hazardous by the loose earth and stones that moved beneath the heavy boots of the laden infantry. About halfway up, an iron fence protruded at right angles to the face of the ridge. As the troops were negotiating this obstacle, a machine-gun opened up but could not bring its fire to bear on them, being dug in to cover the other side of the river. Before too long, the whole company had struggled to the top and set about consolidating the position just as dawn was breaking.

After an eventful night and with the loss of a complete company, the 5th Wiltshires had finally been able to establish themselves on the eastern bank of the River Seine. Although enemy resistance had died away somewhat, this small bridgehead began to look increasingly vulnerable in the gathering light.

It had also been an eventful night for the other assaulting battalion, the 4th Somersets. At around midnight, Colonel Lipscombe had ordered his 'B' Company to go over and land 300 yards (274m) further upstream of his two stranded companies. The new site was nearer the old road bridge and much closer to the village of Vernonnet.

Sitting on board a DUKW, parked in the tree-lined Avenue des Capucins that led down to the river, was Captain J.M.F. Hutchinson. During the earlier fighting in Normandy, he had twice taken over command of the company when his major was wounded. At Vernon he was content to be going forward again, not with the leading platoons as commander, but as follow-up with company HQ. For this battle, at least, he could take a back seat. Unfortunately, events on the river bank were to change all this.

Out of the darkness, he could hear the battalion's second-in-command, Major Brind, marching down the columns of vehicles, calling his name. Realising something was wrong, he jumped down from the DUKW to be greeted with the news that Major Watts had hurt his back in an accident and that Hutchinson would have to lead the company over.

The news came as something of a shock for, secure in the knowledge that he would be in the rear, he had not paid too much attention at the 'orders' group earlier in the evening. He was not too sure exactly where he was going, nor what his objective was.

Major Brind led him down to the river bank. 'You're going in that DUKW,' he said, pointing to a vehicle waiting by the water's edge, 'and you're going to form a bridgehead over there, securing the high ground on the left,' he ordered, nodding across the river into the darkness. Captain Hutchinson peered into the black night. Nothing could be seen; he could only imagine what lay across the river. A little bewildered, he gathered up his maps, climbed into his transport and set off into the unknown.

The Royal Engineers had bulldozed a slipway down to the river for the DUKWs to enter the water. The first one, carrying the bemused company commander, was launched successfully and chugged out into the silent river. The second DUKW promptly grounded at the bottom of the ramp, thus putting it out of action. Every effort to move it came to nothing; it refused to budge, making it impossible for the rest of the party to get their DUKWs into the water. Frantic calls went out for the stormboats to be brought forward again and all the troops debussed from the amphibious vehicles to board the tiny plywood craft. Meanwhile, Hutchinson and his headquarters section carried on over the river, oblivious to the fact that they had become a solo assault against the enemy-held shore. It was fortunate that they ran aground.

'You can't have run aground,' pleaded the captain, 'not here, not now!' Motionless the black DUKW sat in the middle of the empty river, overlooked by the enemy-controlled heights. At any moment Captain Hutchinson expected to see bright lines of tracer snaking through the night sky and smacking into the helpless craft. Try as they might, the DUKW would not move. 'Could they get a rope across? Could they wade across?' asked the captain. 'Oh non, monsieur, très difficile', commented their guide from the Maquis. They would have to get help from the rest of the company, but where were they? Hutchinson looked long and hard into the murky night; all was quiet, nothing could be seen on the river. Finally the awful truth dawned on him that they were alone.

The pandemonium back on the river bank had given way to an orderly line of stormboats, each with a full load of infantry, nosing their way down the river towards the new landing place. As the high-pitched buzz of their engines was heard by the men on the stranded DUKW, the captain jumped up and began signalling to the boats with his lamp. None of his company saw it, or at least if they did they failed to understand its message, thinking perhaps it came from the enemy. The stormboats, all intent on reaching the other side as quickly as possible, all carried on downstream.

The whole situation developed a farcical air when the DUKW's passengers all stood up and began shouting for someone to come and take them off. They were finally rescued by the Royal Engineers piloting the stormboats, after they had heard the plaintive cries. The returning craft then diverted to pick up the stranded men and ferry them over to join the rest of the company, not in the lead as planned, but bringing up the rear. The 4th Somersets had at last made it over the River Seine and on to the mainland the other side.

The company had landed about 150 yards (137m) below the village of Vernonnet on a wide grassy bank that, in more peaceful times, would have made a perfect picnic spot. There had been no opposition directed at the crossing, although sporadic fire was still being aimed from the high ground to the left of the village at the two other companies on the island further downstream.

All was quiet as 'B' Company set about its task of reaching the spur of high ground on the northern end of Vernonnet. The leading platoon wound its way through the gardens and allotments into one of the main streets. It was all supposed to be in silence, but hobnailed boots crunching on slates blown from roofs in the bombardment rather gave the game away.

At the top of the street was a well-camouflaged machine-gun covering the road. When the approaching troops reached the last of the houses, a burst of fire tore into the leading infantry, killing three and wounding several others. Bullets ricocheted off the road and surrounding buildings, pinning down the platoon, who crouched in doorways, searching for cover. Unable to move forward, they waited for assistance from the rest of the company. A frontal attack seemed out of the question. Captain Hutchinson decided to take a few men and move away to the left, in order to encircle the opposition.

They passed back to the edge of the village and then made their way up the hill, through the gardens and orchards behind the houses. Moving as quietly as possible, they came upon another machine-gun post dug into the hill slightly below them. The three Germans manning it were completely unaware of their presence. It appeared that they had no idea that any British troops were over the river, for all three were standing up in the pit, looking out across the Seine towards Vernon.

With two well-placed grenades, the Somersets announced their arrival and then continued through the small alleyways to the top of the village. Another silent approach by one section succeeded in attacking the troublesome machine-gun at the top of the main street, knocking it out and killing the crew.

Captain Hutchinson paused for a while, sitting on the stone wall beside the knocked-out German gun, and pondered the situation. The enemy was obviously in Vernonnet in some strength and it would not be safe to move out and attack the high ground until the houses and gardens on the northern edge of the village were cleared. In the darkness, Hutchinson set his platoons the difficult and dangerous task of moving through the buildings, flushing out snipers and other pockets of resistance. Fortunately, they were soon assisted by 'D' Company, which had crossed the river behind them, so that by dawn the 4th Somersets were in command of the side of Vernonnet that lay beneath the left-hand escarpment. They had bagged a great many prisoners from the German 148 Grenadier Regiment, most of whom were quite happy to give themselves up without too much of a fight.

At about the same time, the opposite, southern end of Vernonnet was being cleared by 'D' Company of the 5th Wiltshires, who had moved down the valley to secure the bridging sites and had continued into the village.

Just as dawn was breaking, silent, dark figures from a new formation moved cautiously from doorway to doorway through the centre of Vernonnet. They were men from the 1st Worcestershires who had made their way over the Seine dry-shod, across the ruins of the old stone road bridge.

After their rebuff on the old Pont de Vernon the previous evening, the battalion had withdrawn to the crypt of the local cathedral for a hot meal and some rest. With the pillbox on the far end of the bridge still intact, it was suicidal to attempt another crossing. A six-pounder anti-tank gun was brought up to the river with a view to pounding the offending machine-gun post by the light of parachute flares, but this project was abandoned when news came through that the 5th Wiltshires were attempting to take the far exit of the bridge and could be caught in the line of fire.

Watching all this activity on the river bank was Sergeant G.R. Butcher, a section commander with the 4th Wiltshires. He and his men had been digging slit trenches in the garden of a large house right opposite the entrance to the old bridge since the previous afternoon, their task being to prevent any enemy infiltration across its broken spans.

Butcher had seen the assaults on both flanks and had witnessed the pitiless machine-gunning of the men from the 5th Wiltshires as they struggled in the water. He went to the aid of a wounded sergeant who was floating downstream with the dead bodies, and was all the while conscious of the German guns overlooking the site. Together with two engineers, he toiled up the steep bank with the injured man, keeping a watchful eye over his shoulder for any signs of interference from the enemy. The rescue attempt was not fired on, perhaps as an act of compassion.

As the night wore on, no more news arrived of events on the other side, nor indeed could any sound of firing be heard to indicate that the 5th Wiltshires had reached the Vernonnet end of the old bridge. The pressing need to have more men over the river before daylight led to the decision that the 1st Worcestershires should once again attempt to force the bridge.

The men of 'A' Company were roused from their sleep and filed down to the river bank. Under the cover of a little smoke from their own mortars, the leading men once again climbed the ladder on to the first broken span. This time they had a good idea of what to expect. Warily the leading platoon crept over the twisted remains and negotiated the booby-trapped road block, expecting that at any moment they would be caught by the fire from the pillbox covering the end of the bridge.

To everyone's astonishment and relief, there was no resistance whatsoever; the enemy had gone. The threat to their rear from the troops already over had prompted them to withdraw. The Germans were evidently prepared to man a machine-gun post on the exposed end of the bridge in darkness, but thought it an entirely different proposition in daylight, at the mercy of heavy shelling and infiltration from behind.

Soon other men of the battalion were hurrying across and into the village, preparing to move towards their original objective of the previous evening: the high ground behind the centre of Vernonnet.

Throughout the night, whilst the infantry had been attempting to establish themselves on the enemy-held far shore, the Royal Engineers had been busy with their own great task: that of bridging the Seine.

The first of the division's bridges over the river was to be constructed by its own group of engineers. Lieutenant-Colonel Evill gave the job of erecting this Class 9 folding boat equipment bridge to two of his field companies: 553 and 204. It was to be suitable for wheeled vehicles of up to 9 tons (able to carry lorries and carriers, but not tanks). The whole structure was made up in sections, each length of roadway being supported by four boats. These sections were assembled away from the bridging site and then towed up–river into position, to be connected up to others to form the main body of the bridge. At each end of the bridge was a half-floating bay, clamped to a trestle, which in turn was fixed to the shore. Small ramps led on and off the bridge.

The site chosen for the Class 9 bridge was about ninety yards (82m) upstream of the demolished road bridge. There was a good access to the near end from the town and on the far side; its exit led onto a lane running up from the river into Vernonnet. A great deal of earth-moving was needed to lessen the steep slope down to the water. In addition, a masonry wall had to be demolished on the edge of the river to allow a steady gradient for the approach to the bridge.

As the first waves of the initial assault took to the water at H-Hour, the two field companies began moving into the harbouring area in the streets just behind the waterfront. With them was the RASC transport carrying the bridging equipment. They had been told that speed was essential and that bridging would begin as soon as possible. In a short while, reconnaissance parties brought back news of the disasters affecting the Wiltshires and the start was postponed. After about two hours, in which time the commander had been unable to get any more information concerning the happenings on the left of the Wiltshires' bridgehead (the area which mainly covered the proposed bridging site), Lieutenant-Colonel Evill requested the brigade commander's permission to start building.

At 2215 hours, Brigadier Mole agreed to let the sappers begin. This was probably a little premature, as at that time the opposite side was still firmly controlled by the enemy. The 5th Wiltshires had only one company across the river, way over to the right, about half-a-mile upstream.

The first job attempted by the engineers was to clear the site and its approaches on the near bank. Armoured bulldozers gradually manoeuvred their way down to the river's edge. The roar of their engines brought down a shower of mortar bombs on the construction site, and from across the water a machine-gun opened up, firing down the line of the proposed bridge. Every attempt to clear the site to provide the approach road was met with intense resistance. Shells began to fall onto the unfortunate sappers, forcing them to halt their work and take cover. The Germans had realised immediately the significance of the work in progress and were determined to stop any attempt at bridging. In this they were successful, for the engineers backed away from the river to await the clearance of the far bank.

About one hundred yards (91m) below the old bridge, the near shore was partially hidden from view from the opposite bank by a tree-covered island. The folding boats, with their sections of roadway that went to make up the bridge, were assembled here. Out of sight of the enemy, they were later moored under the lee of the island in mid-river, to await the completion of the approaches and landing bays upstream.

Although this short length of the waterfront was not in full view of the enemy, it was, nonetheless, a difficult task for anyone to approach the area unseen. Cliff Roberts, a driver with 553 Field Company, remembers the awkward process of getting his truckload of bridging equipment safely to the river:

The construction site was still under shell-fire. My truck had to be led through the town and down to the Seine. Sergeant Welland guided me along the main street which was itself still under sniper fire. He walked about sixty yards in front of my lorry. If he crossed the road, I had to do the same at precisely that point. If he carried on along the pavement, I drove down the pavement behind him. When we got to the end of the road near the site, he directed me into an area at the back of a café surrounded by a high wall. When the sappers arrived to pick up the boats, they were not very happy; there was still some distance to be covered before they reached the water's edge. They had to manhandle the cumbersome rafts around the back gardens of some houses to get them down to the river. Once out in the open, they were forced to creep forward behind the cover of an armoured bulldozer in an effort to escape sniper fire. Whilst my truck was being unloaded, a house close by received a direct hit from a salvo of enemy shells which killed two medics inside and covered me with debris. Outside, just behind the wall, other sappers suffered badly; one lost an arm and a leg. The atmosphere was electric.

Throughout the night, the engineers continued to build the thirty-five rafts needed for the bridge (the boats and sections of roadway were called rafts by the sappers). Even in this relatively sheltered spot, the work was continually interrupted and casualties were suffered by both men and rafts from the intermittent shelling. German anti-aircraft guns high up on the far hills sent lines of tracer shells to probe the area of the near bank. Although the leader of one of the building parties was killed on his raft, work still continued at a furious pace so as to enable the engineers to be ready to continue with the construction of the bridge proper, once the far shore had been cleared.

At one point during the night, all work came to a halt for a short time when boatloads of wounded infantry from the 4th Somersets were brought back across the river and all hands went to help the injured ashore. By 0345 hours, the rafts were all completed and moored close to the island in midstream, to await the recommencement of the bridge building.

As for the men captured the previous night, the fighting was all over. They looked a sorry sight as they marched away into captivity. The Germans could not believe that the bloodstained and dishevelled Major Milne was indeed an officer. Although he had been badly wounded in the hand, he was covered in blood from head to foot (most of it not his own). The enemy thought he was seriously injured, but it was just as well he was not, as Vic Coombs found out after carrying his dead German all the way back to a field hospital. There were virtually no medical supplies available. The captured men all gave their field dressings to a doctor, who was very grateful for them.

Signaller Fred Greenwood had a most curious experience when confronted by a German Intelligence officer. He was accused of belonging to a regiment of shock-troops. The officer suggested that the 5th Royal Berkshires (to whom Signaller Greenwood belonged) had landed on the invasion beaches and were now storm-troops for the Seine crossing. This amused Greenwood, for although it was true that he had landed at H-Hour plus 45 minutes on D-Day, the 5th Berkshires were there to provide the signals. After their task was finished, they were split up and sent to other units, four of them being attached to the 5th Wiltshires. All of his denials were in vain; that German officer was convinced that the 5th Royal Berkshire Regiment was composed of storm-troopers who were used for special assaults.

Later that day, the men were lined up and force-marched away from the battle. They walked about thirty miles (48km) a day until they arrived in Amiens, where they were loaded onto cattle trucks. The train pulled out of the station to the sound of gunfire from just outside the town. The Allies were not far behind them; a few more hours and they might have been freed. As it was, they began a frightening train journey across Europe into captivity, made worse by the complete dominance of the air by the Allied Air Forces.

The train was subjected to an attack by rocket-firing Typhoon aircraft, during which the German guards fled, leaving their prisoners trapped in the trucks until the raid was over. Later, in the Frankfurt marshalling yard, locked in the flimsy wooden wagons, the helpless captives had to survive a terrifying raid by the RAF. As one of them later recalled, 'It was the closest thing to hell on earth that anyone is likely to endure.'

Situation at 0500 Hours Saturday 26 August

It was now daylight and ten hours had elapsed since the start of the assault. The battle was falling dramatically behind schedule. None of the original objectives had been reached:

The 5th Wiltshires were at last over the river, but had suffered the loss of an entire company. The battalion had blocked the road leading down the valley to the enemy, but its troops were now only just beginning to clear the southern end of Vernonnet and make the area ready for bridging operations.

In the middle of the village, the 1st Worcestershires were rooting out the newly arrived German 1 Battalion 148 Grenadier Regiment and preparing to move on to the central spur behind Vernonnet as soon as the buildings were clear of the enemy.

The 4th Somerset Light Infantry had only two companies across and were still trying to clear the northern side of the village. As soon as this was done, they were to move against their main objective, the downstream spur overlooking the Royal Engineers bridge assembly area.

The division was still well short of where it had planned to be at this hour.

Chapter 10

Morning, 26 August

The early morning sun began to expose the enormity of the problems facing the division. Daylight revealed just how small the bridgehead was, gained after a night of fighting. The lodgement area controlled about a mile of the river valley, but nowhere was it more than a few hundred yards deep. The three spurs overlooking the crossing site were still firmly in enemy hands (although one company of the 5th Wiltshires was superimposed on the end of the right-hand escarpment upstream of Vernonnet). None of the three battalions over the river was complete, nor did they possess any anti-tank guns; and the advantage that darkness affords the attacker had been lost.

The division had planned to be well inland and have a Class 9 bridge over the Seine by morning, but it was still strung out along the river bank, with only the demolished stone bridge linking it with Vernon. To the Royal Engineers, the new dawn brought with it the awesome task of bridging the river in daylight, the enemy watching their every move. They could expect continual harassment from machine-guns and snipers; it was a daunting prospect.

The critical nature of the situation was not lost on General Thomas. As he looked across the wide, lazy river, his eyes were drawn to the long spurs of high ground radiating out from Vernonnet. The densely wooded cliffs opposite barred his way inland. Well-established enemy strongpoints remained untouched by the deluge of fire that had been thrown across the river the previous night and, as the valley emerged from the darkness, the Spandaus once again started up defiantly, punishing any open movement on the near bank. The threat from their fire was as formidable as it had been twelve hours earlier. It would remain so until the British infantry had swept along each high bluff and cleared them out.

Thomas needed more troops over the river, and quickly. Even as he watched, the follow-up companies of the 1st Worcestershires were scrambling across the ruined Pont de Vernon. He decided that once Vernonnet had been completely cleared of the enemy, the 4th Wiltshires would cross over the ruined bridge and move up the river valley to help clear the long cliff, to the right of Vernonnet, that dominated the bridging sites. Their task of close protection of Vernon now looked to be unnecessary, for there had been no enemy interference from the north on that side of the river. Nevertheless, ever cautious as he was, he ordered tanks of the 15th/19th Royal Hussars, together with 'C' Squadron of the 43rd Reconnaissance Regiment, to carry out an offensive sweep down the river valley to confirm that the area was clear of Germans. This done, the left flank could be forgotten and his attention concentrated on the problems across the river.

With his small lodgement vulnerable to any concerted counter-attack, Thomas also needed anti-tank guns over with the leading battalions. Close-support rafts had been built during the night to transport these weapons across, but had not been employed because of the confusion on the far bank. Thomas now ordered ferrying operations to begin.

The right-hand ferry site had its landing place on the far shore covered by the 5th Wiltshires' bridgehead and so was able to begin operations within a short space of time. The raft was not, unfortunately, an immediate success. Continual enemy interference interrupted each trip and it took the whole morning to get just three guns and three carriers over. The process proved to be both slow and dangerous on this stretch of the river.

The Class 9 raft on the left of the division's positions below the old bridge had its proposed landing site in the area controlled by the 4th Somersets. However, that section of the opposite bank close to Vernonnet still appeared to hold pockets of the enemy. Knowledge of the area was a little sketchy and, as the riverside there needed surveying, a party of the Royal Engineers was sent over to investigate.

Sergeant Rex Hunt from 260 Field Company was again selected to lead a team across the river to check out the far shore. The previous evening he had gone across to reconnoitre the cut between the 4th Somersets' island and the mainland. This time things were a little quieter; his party loaded onto a stormboat and made for the mainland opposite, upstream of the large island.

The small boat had almost reached the far side when the events of the night before started to repeat themselves. The craft came under fire from a machine-gun set back in some trees a little further up-river. Almost immediately the helmsman was hit as he crouched low over the outboard motor in an effort to escape the firing. Blood began to pour from his neck and shoulder. Before anyone could grab the tiller, the boat veered sideways and crashed into the bank of a small island, spilling the occupants out onto the shore in an ungainly pile. Fortunately, none of the passengers was injured, either by the sudden halt, or by the enemy fire. The shaken men were all able to pick themselves up and crawl along the muddy bank and into some trees.

Unintentionally, Sergeant Hunt had again found himself to be on an island. This time, he was determined to find a way off quickly. He led his party through the trees towards the backwater separating the island from the mainland. They had only gone a short distance when they came across a German soldier crouched in a slit trench, manning a light machine-gun. The poor man was almost as startled as the engineers by the sudden confrontation. He made no attempt to fire his gun and quickly put up his hands in surrender. A few moments later, another enemy soldier was found nearby. He, too, rid himself of his weapon and gave up the fight without firing a shot. These two enemy soldiers had been on the island under cover all night. Bypassed by the 4th Somersets, they had continued to interfere with activities on that part of the river without drawing attention to themselves. They now seemed quite happy to surrender to the first British troops they came across.

The survey team pressed on and crossed over the small muddy backwater to reach the mainland. They then moved upstream along the river bank, searching for a place for the rafts to land. The only suitable spot for an off-loading site was just fifty yards (45m) short of the old road bridge. By this time it was mid-morning and any activity on the river was attracting enemy attention. Reluctantly, orders were given to postpone the start of ferrying until the shooting had eased.

As daylight came, early that morning, the divisional artillery once again began to place smoke shells onto the hills on the far side of the Seine. Mortars along the river-front joined in, helping to shield the town from enemy view. With such a large area to cover, it was difficult to keep the river banks continually shrouded in this protective mist. For, as is the nature of smoke, it began drifting about on any slight breeze, permeating every space and polluting the air with its acrid fumes. At times, the whole town of Vernon would disappear beneath this silent blanket, only to suddenly re-emerge into the warm sunshine and be greeted by the whine and roar of a shell from the other side of the river. It took a prodigious amount of smoke shells to maintain this screen and by mid-morning supplies were all but exhausted.

At around 0900 hours, work recommenced on the Class 9 folding boat bridge, codenamed DAVID. The opposite landing point was at last in friendly hands and hopes were high for a speedy completion. Two armoured bulldozers lumbered from their hiding places behind the houses along the riverside where they had sought shelter the night before. As the sound of their engines drifted across the water, the enemy on the far hills once again renewed efforts to interfere with the work. Shells and mortar bombs plunged down through the smoke, in an attempt to seek out the source of the labouring noise. Machine-gun fire added to the hazards faced by the sappers as they set about clearing the area by the river, ready for the bridge-building. Within an hour, after several interruptions and some casualties, construction work on the near bank had been completed. Orders were passed down the river to begin the transportation of the assembled rafts, with their sections of roadway, up to the bridging site.

The rafts had been moored in mid-stream behind an island, away from the enemy's sporadic fire. Thirty-five rafts had been built, but two had vanished. The men detailed to moor them had been killed, the rafts drifting away unseen into the night.

Two of the division's field companies, 553 and 204, now began the dangerous task of bringing the component parts of the bridge together under enemy fire. Below the old demolished road bridge, the shoreline near the anchored rafts was turning out to be a particularly exposed place. The raft-building site was immediately opposite the spur that the 4th Somersets were hoping to clear. Several machine-guns and anti-aircraft cannon on the hill overlooking the site kept any movement to a minimum. There were, however, occasional quiet spells in this interdictory fire. From time to time, the enemy's attention was diverted to deal with the Somersets, scrambling about on the slopes below them, who were set on taking the heights. During one such lull, the sappers took to the water and towed the first six rafts up the river, beneath the undamaged arches of the ruined bridge and into position some ninety yards further on. This brought them on to the section of water immediately under the long spur to the right of Vernonnet. Machine-guns and snipers were waiting for them. Through the patchy smoke-screen the enemy opened fire; the exposed rafts were an easy target.

Bullets began to strike the wooden boats and road-bearing panels. There was no cover, no hiding place, for the sappers crouched low in the slim craft. With shirt-sleeves rolled up and head bowed low, each engineer carried on, intent on completing his task. Unarmed and having only a steel helmet for protection, they could not have the satisfaction of returning fire to ease their frustration. They had to suffer all that was thrown at them. Inevitably, the number of casualties began to mount. Within a few minutes there were only a few men left alive or uninjured.

Sergeant Hick's raft was peppered with bullets in mid-stream, but he pressed on and manoeuvred his craft into position. Then, sending all but two of the crew ashore, he struggled on through the hail of fire to fix the connectors. His defiant stance helped to inspire the men on other rafts and those watching from the relative safety of both banks.

Just a short distance from the landing site on the far shore, the 5th Wiltshires had set up their battalion HQ. It was situated in the 'V' formed by two felled trees, where a hole had been dug and sandbagged into a secure base. From the safety of this well-protected, almost comfortable hole, one of the battalion's signallers, Ken Burroughs, looked out onto this life and death struggle taking place below him on the river. To him, those Royal Engineers were some of the bravest men he had ever seen and he was filled with admiration for them. He saw the sappers being picked off, one by one, as they swung their unwieldy craft into line and set about connecting them together. Yet still more came up, each new craft slipping under the masonry arches of the old bridge and into the fierce fire. With perfect discipline they pressed on with the job in hand. The long, hard, boring exercises they had endured back in England, the bridging and re-bridging of the rivers of Kent, were all suffered in preparation for this day. They were bridging one of the major rivers of Europe, in daylight, under fire. It was their finest hour.

The enemy, for their part, were equally determined that the bridge should not be built. All of their attention was now focused on this small stretch of river and the activities on each adjacent bank. In reply, every available weapon in the Wessex Division let loose a barrage of retaliatory fire. Behind every trigger there was a man equally determined to give aid to his comrades out in the exposed centre of the river. The cross-fire rose to a crescendo as each side sought to frustrate the other's intentions. It was a struggle in which victory, temporarily, went to the enemy. The casualties being suffered by the highly trained engineers and their equipment forced Lieutenant-Colonel Evill to call a halt to the work. It was a bitter blow to the division. The bridge was desperately needed to speed more troops into the bridgehead. The decision was, however, inevitable; there could be no further work on the river until the high ground had been cleared of the enemy.

Since dawn, elements of three battalions had been continuing their efforts to clear Vernonnet completely. When they were sure that the village was safe, each intended to move out and attack the three main spurs overlooking the river: the 5th Wiltshires to the south opposite Vernon, the 1st Worcestershires to the east behind the village and the 4th Somersets to the north.

Daylight found Captain Hutchinson and 'B' Company of the 4th Somerset Light Infantry at the northern end of Vernonnet beneath the steep chalky slopes of the high spur. From the top of the cliffs the enemy continued their harassing fire directed at the Royal Engineers' raft-building site. Fortunately, by this time, the Somersets' two stranded companies had been re-embarked from their island and had landed in the village without too much trouble. Nonetheless, the Germans on the hill had not been too preoccupied with the Vernon side of the river to notice the Somersets below them in the village. When 'B' Company tried to move out of the gardens and allotments and onto the slopes of the ridge, the enemy reacted sharply with machine-guns and small cannon, forcing them back.

To Captain Hutchinson, looking up at the defended heights, the cliffs seemed impregnable now that daylight had arrived. A frontal attack was likely to prove costly. Colonel Lipscombe decided to see if the spur could be turned from the rear and so, whilst his three remaining companies kept the Germans busy with fire from the village, Lipscombe sent 'D' Company to fight its way out of the village up the Gisors road and try to get on to the back of the cliffs.

The first of the Worcestershires' companies to cross the ruined Pont de Vernon was 'A' Company. They immediately set about forming a defensive perimeter around its exit for the others to pass through. In so doing, Private Ken Lugg, together with some others of his platoon, chased a few Germans into a building that looked rather like a small café. Lugg was all for going in and flushing them out, but was told to dig in and leave it to the artillery. The men of his section fell back and dropped down in a flower-bed, scratching themselves shallow slit trenches for cover. It was just as well they did, for when the shells came over the building in front of them disintegrated. Debris and rubble filled the air, silencing the elusive party of Germans.

Between the bridge and the eastern end of Vernonnet, there were still some enemy infantry skilfully hidden in gardens and behind walls, waiting for the advancing Worcestershiremen. Leading the movement through the village was a section containing Private D. Hodgkins. As this group rounded a corner, they were greeted by a burst of light machine-gun fire from a concealed enemy post. The over-anxious German operating the gun sent all his fire high and wide, leaving the startled section time to disappear back round the corner. Hodgkins, with a couple of the others, ducked into a house close by and made for an upstairs window. From their vantage point, they could see the enemy machine-gun exposed below them. A concentrated burst from their guns killed the enemy crew, who were all still looking intently at the corner round which the Wessexmen had retreated.

Little more opposition was met with in the village; those Germans who were left quickly gave themselves up. The resistance encountered in Vernonnet had been, for the most part, not too determined. Although a few casualties had been taken by the division in capturing the village, there had been none of the delays and complications that had been envisaged during the planning stages from fighting in the built-up area so soon after landing.

The battalion of the German 148th Grenadier Regiment that had arrived during the night had immediately found itself in action. This first taste of battle, experienced by what were largely units made up of foreigners, was not welcomed. They found that instead of marching to the river to relieve troops guarding the Seine, they had walked into a full-scale battle. Those of them who moved out onto the spurs overlooking the water kept up a brave stance with sniper and machine-gun fire, but those left in Vernonnet came face to face in the dark with determined troops intent on taking the village. This called for an equally determined stance by themselves, but these 'German' troops, conscripted to fight for a country that was not their own, were unable to provide it.

'B' Company of the 1st Worcestershires, commanded by Major Algy Grubb, now crossed over the ruined bridge into the recently secured Vernonnet. Major Grubb's orders were to pass through the other company and push on up the spur of high ground behind the village. He was instructed to advance along a track to the right of the church. As he recalls, he was 'lousy at following maps':

My trouble was this: I was perfectly capable of reading a map, but I rarely believed it. Somehow I always went in the wrong direction. I did not believe that the track by the church was the one that the colonel intended me to go up, it did not seem to go anywhere. There was this nice little road going up the side of the hill and I thought, 'That's it, he's got it wrong', for the object of the exercise was to get on the top of the high ground. The road I took went round some houses and then led out of the village. It wasn't long before I realised that I was on the wrong route, but what was I to do then? It was no good turning back, I decided to go on and hope for the best.

Grubb could see his objective, the high ground away to the left, and felt that he could carry on and then cut across to the spur from the flank. What he did not take into account was that as he went further up the road, the ground on the left dropped away alarmingly. He was now on the wrong spur, having ventured onto the back of the escarpment overlooking the bridging sites. He had strayed into the 5th Wiltshires' territory, advancing along the road that led to La Chapelle St Ouen.

The 5th Wiltshires were somewhere up on my right, but were nowhere to be seen. I carried on along the road, which bore round to the left at the edge of Vernonnet and then continued straight for a few hundred yards. We were advancing in two columns, one on either side of the road. As we approached the end of the straight, an enemy machine-gun opened up on the leading troops.

The German gun was situated in a fork in the road formed by its junction with a lane that led to Bois Jérôme. In the centre of the leading section was a Bren gunner, Private Albert Kings. The fire from the enemy Spandau hit the two lines of British infantry with complete surprise and Kings immediately heard a cry from someone close behind who had been hit. In a moment, everyone had gone to ground on either side of the road.

Kings was hidden from the enemy by a hump in the grass verge. Lying in a ditch by the side of the road a few feet away was Bert Smith. He was wounded and calling for stretcher-bearers. In no time, two bearers came ambling up the road to help. Kings was struck by the way the two medics worked in full view of the enemy, armed only with Red Cross flags. They lifted the wounded private onto the stretcher and raised him up. Then something happened that those watching would never forget: the machine-gun opened fire on the three men in the road, killing them all instantly.

The troops crouching by the roadside were furious, but the continual firing from the offending gun forced them to keep their heads down. As the gunfire swept up and down the road, it sprayed the verges with a stream of bullets, catching any man not fortunate enough to be completely concealed. Across the road from Private Kings, his best friend Joe Cartwright was killed in this hail of fire.

The leading troops were pinned down, unable to move. Towards the rear, Grubb had realised the situation was becoming critical; his men were gradually being picked off as they lay with their faces pressed into the earth. Just a short way back down the road nearer Vernonnet was a narrow lane that led up into a chalk quarry cut in the face of the cliffs. Grubb decided to send an officer and a few men up this lane to try to outflank the enemy gun.

After the losses the company had suffered in Normandy, Major Grubb had only one officer available to use. His name was Rex Fellows. As Grubb explains: 'He was a good chap, but being new to the company, he was "red raw".' Fellows had joined the company just over a week earlier at Berjou and the major was rather concerned that it took a little time to get used to this sort of business. There was, however, no alternative; the young officer had to be used. Fellows was ordered to take his platoon up the lane, move through the undergrowth to a position above the Spandau and rush the gun across the main road.

Grubb need not have had any cause for concern: Fellows did the job magnificently. The whole scheme worked to perfection. A textbook attack was put in, only to find the enemy had retired through the trees to new positions a short way up the road. By this time, the Worcestershires were eager for revenge after the atrocity with the stretcher-bearers, but this was to be denied them. For, as they consolidated near the fork in the road, mortar bombs started to fall all around them, forcing them once again to take cover. Clearly a strong enemy force had been concealed in the thick undergrowth at the road junction and it was now carrying out a rearguard action of some competence.

The company was forced to halt in rather an awkward place for there was little room to deploy: to their right there were the high cliffs on the side of the spur overlooking the river, to their left the ground fell away sharply, ahead was apparently a considerable number of the enemy dug in, blocking any advance, and all around them was the thick, closely knit countryside, with visibility down to just a few yards.

There then followed a total lull and, as so often happens on such occasions, there was a momentary relaxation of concentration. Sergeant Kerrigan and another man who had recently joined the company took themselves off into the chalkpit to relieve themselves. At the same time, to his amazement, Grubb saw, striding up the road from the direction of Vernonnet, Lieutenant-Colonel Bill Roberts, commander of the 5th Wiltshires. They were old friends. Roberts saw Algy Grubb lying in the ditch by the side of the road and, with a big smile on his face, exclaimed to him jokingly, 'Bloody hell, what are you doing here!' Whilst he was getting information on the Worcestershires' predicament, standing all the while in full view on the road, he was interrupted by enemy fire which began to hit the road surface all around him. With chippings jumping up literally around his feet, he turned his face up to the cliffs and said, 'That's bloody rude!' He then turned and walked off back down the road as though nothing had happened.

What had happened was that an enemy force had filtered along the high ground on the company's right. This was the rear face of the spur that the 5th Wiltshires were to operate, but at that time they were still at the front of the escarpment awaiting reinforcements. It subsequently transpired that this same enemy force had killed Sergeant Kerrigan in the chalkpit; they had shot him through the head.

Clearly the company was now in danger of being outflanked. Major Grubb therefore decided to regain the initiative and remove from the high ground those Germans who were overlooking him. With a small party he made his way up to the top of the bluff, but found the Germans had gone. The thickly wooded plateau on top of the spur did not allow any pursuit by his small force. He left a patrol in position and returned to his main force.

'B' Company had lost five men killed in this little action, and Grubb decided that he was not going to lose any more in this difficult terrain. He therefore established his company in good positions astride the road, to await the time when the 5th Wiltshires had moved sufficient distance inland on the high ground to protect his flank. He could then, depending on circumstances, either attack the enemy up the main road or move over to the left to rejoin his battalion. Until that time, he would make sure no Germans moved back down the road towards the river.

Just after daybreak, as the main body of the Worcestershires was scrambling over the old bridge, Lieutenant Holly and his company of the 5th Wiltshires were resting on top of the escarpment, looking out towards Vernon. After their exhausting climb in the dark, they had dug themselves some protection against their position on the extreme end of this spur next to Vernonnet. In the light of day their small enclave looked vulnerable. Away to their left the long cliffs that stretch upstream were still riddled with enemy machine-gun posts and snipers. Behind them, the thick woods on top of the spur were just a few yards from their trenches. The most exposed of all the British troops over the river, they nervously awaited an enemy reaction to their presence.

This one company of infantry was not strong enough to sweep along the high ground without support, but the rest of the battalion was occupied elsewhere: 'D' Company was in Vernonnet and 'B' Company was holding the road along the river valley. Until the 4th Wiltshires had crossed the river, no further progress could be made in clearing the cliffs of the enemy opposition that was causing such havoc with the bridge-building.

As soon as the news of the 1st Worcestershires' progress through Vernonnet was received back in Vernon, the 4th Wiltshires formed up and filed down to the water. Moving one company at a time, the battalion crossed the old bridge into the lodgement area. Its transfer across the river passed unmolested by the Germans, who at that time were giving their full attention to the work of the Royal Engineers in mid-stream.

Major Dim Robbins had spent the night in comfortable lodgings (gained once again for him by his gallant second-in-command, Captain Chrisp), but sleep had not come easily. 'C' Company was in reserve for the assault, situated around the battalion HQ near the railway station. Earlier on during the attack, news began to filter back of the troubles the 5th Wiltshires were suffering and, as the night wore on, the news became even more alarming. It was a worrying time, as Major Robbins explains:

When you are in reserve, you tend to conserve your strength and think, 'What's the worst thing now that could happen to me? If the Germans capture the assault companies I could be asked to go and retrieve the position. 1 could even be asked to swim the river, should all the boats go down!' As it happened, 1 was not asked to do anything that night and did not have to go over the river until mid-morning the next day.

When Robbins and his company reached the far side of the bridge, they turned right and moved up the river valley along the road that ran beneath the cliffs. They soon arrived among their sister battalion, the 5th Wiltshires, passing through their 'B' Company to reach the house which, only a few hours earlier that morning, had been the headquarters of the vanquished 'A' Company. The depressing debris from the night's fighting lay all around, slowly decaying in the hot August sunshine.

These reinforcements, arriving at the base of the spur, now released 'B' Company to join those others of the 5th Wiltshires on top of the escarpment. Together the two companies moved into the woods and began the slow, laborious task of clearing the dense plateau of any enemy. The 4th Wiltshires continued southwards, sweeping along the hillside on a three-company front: 'A' Company on the top, 'B' Company on the precipitous face and 'C' Company along the bottom, all trying to flush out the troublesome enemy from their well-established machine-gun posts.

Back across the river in Vernon, the French civilians were becoming a little more confident as the streets and alleyways began to fill with troops waiting to go over. An occasional shell or two fell on the town and sent everyone scurrying for cover, but the joy they felt at being liberated overcame their fear and they were soon thronging around the waiting vehicles once again. The smoke-screen continued to drift back and forth over the town and, with all the English voices shouting up and down the lines of trucks, Jacques Cambuza imagined himself to be in a London smog.

It had been a good year for fruit in Monsieur Cambuza's garden. He had a great crop of tomatoes and wished to share some of them with the English soldiers. Parked a short distance away from his house was a line of trucks, loaded with sections of Bailey bridge, belonging to the Royal Engineers. He approached some of the troops and was immediately impressed with their sense of order and discipline, for, instead of accepting the tomatoes, they took him to see their officer. He repeated his offer once again and the officer accepted. A few moments later, he returned with about twenty kilos of fruit, much to the delight of the troops. The cook straightaway cut them up and dished them out to the men. It was the first fresh food they had eaten in a long while. In return, the cook packed Cambuza's bags full of all kinds of tins, things that were quite unthinkable to the French at that time, and he staggered back to his family absolutely loaded down with items that they had been deprived of for four years. To this day, he still proudly shows an unopened tin of fifty NAAFI issue cigarettes, as a reminder of the generosity of those British troops.

On the outskirts of Vernon, by the side of the road that winds round the grounds of the Château de Bizy, Major Michael Concannon had left the artillery positions of the 94th Field Regiment and was watching the arrival of the Royal Engineers' equipment into the town. Being well back from the river, a large number of French civilians had turned out to see the British troops coming in. There was a great deal of transport carrying, road-building and huge excavating equipment, the like of which the French had never seen. The people were all cheering and waving as these monstrous machines went by. The sheer bulk of the forces amazed the jubilant crowds. Although not a French scholar, Michael Concannon recognised one word that was repeated over and over: 'for-me-dah-ble!'

In the Vernon area, the civilians appeared different from those so far seen elsewhere; they seemed to be much more sophisticated, of more Parisian character. Major Concannon recalls that this was immediately evident to the troops and they reacted to it:

> They had not got on too well with the Normandy people, who hadn't come up to their expectations of going to France. I think a lot of men expected a kind of 'La Vie Parisienne' type, but they didn't get that in Normandy. The Normans were a dour people. Of course the troops were welcomed and were quite well looked after, but there wasn't the glamour of the 'French Girl' about them. Then there was the destruction that had taken place in Normandy; that made the men feel rather guilty. In Vernon, however, things were different; in Vernon, they were the conquering heroes.

Also indulging in the role of 'liberators' was 'C' Squadron of the 43rd Reconnaissance Regiment. Together with tanks of the 15th/19th Royal Hussars, they were sweeping the area north of Vernon, between the Eure and the Seine. Sergeant George Drake and his troop of armoured cars had arrived in the village of Venables, which was situated in a large loop of the Seine, opposite Les Andelys. They were met by a very enthusiastic band of the FFI, armed to the teeth and looking like bandits.

Drake climbed to the top of the tower of the local church to spy out the land. Surrounding the village were very thickly wooded hills and nothing could be seen but the trees. The resistance men were sure that there were German tanks in those nearby woods, immobilised owing to a lack of petrol. The French were so insistent that the troop leader agreed to allow his men to take the armoured cars and have a look. With one of the Frenchmen on the top of his car to act as guide, Drake led the troop of cars down a leafy lane and into the woods.

As quietly as possible, the rubber-wheeled vehicles advanced cautiously through the sunlit trees, stopping from time to time to listen for signs of the enemy. After one such pause, Drake spotted a lone German soldier lying, apparently asleep, under a tree. The poor man looked absolutely exhausted. Drake ordered his driver to stop and began to get out of his turret, pistol at the ready. For a moment he had forgotten about his passenger on the back of the car, but the Frenchman had also spotted the sleeping German and, before Drake could stop him, loosed off a complete magazine of Sten gun fire at the surprised enemy, missing him completely. Drake was at that moment half-in and half-out of the turret, which suddenly began to traverse as the gunner looked for the opposition. Thinking they were under attack, the other cars joined in with their own fire and the woods echoed with the sound of battle. The German ran off through the trees like a startled stag and disappeared from view.

It took a long time before order was restored. Sergeant Drake then took the necessary steps to ensure that his passenger had no more ammunition and the cars continued through the forest. There were no tanks of course; there probably never were. Looking back on the event, Drake would like to think the German survived the war after such a rude awakening.

With the infantry on the other side of the river now beginning to secure the lodgement, it was time for Thomas to introduce his second brigade into the action. 214 Brigade, less the 1st Worcestershires who had travelled forward with the Assault Group, had arrived in the area the previous night and was now camped, ready for action, just outside the town.

Six miles short of Vernon, in a large wood just outside Pacy, was the harbouring area for the 5th Duke of Cornwall's Light Infantry. The commanding officer, Lieutenant-Colonel George Taylor, awoke early that Saturday morning, refreshed after a peaceful night's sleep. The previous evening he had been given a forecast for the day's operations. He was to take his battalion over the newly erected boat bridge and become the lead for 214 Brigade's advance through the Forest of Vernon that stretched between Vernonnet and Panilleuse. However, with the new day had come the news of the setbacks suffered during the assault. There was no new bridge, nor could there be any advance out of Vernonnet until the cliffs opposite had been cleared of the enemy. The battalion would have to postpone its move into the town until operations on the other side of the river were under control.

George Taylor was a dedicated and professional soldier. He was a man of immense energy and full of innovation. He had once played rugby for the Barbarians and would have undoubtedly played for England had not his army career intervened. Not content to await events, he decided to instigate his own operations.

Unique to his battalion, as far as the division was concerned, he had created a scout platoon, with two officers and seventeen men, which was used solely for reconnaissance. When not employed for scouting, they formed a useful reserve stationed around battalion HQ. Taylor never used them on fighting patrols, believing this to be rather wasteful of their special talents. They travelled in jeeps, but worked mostly on foot. Heavily armed, they served as the eyes and ears of the battalion.

Taylor now ordered Captain Spencer to take this platoon across the river, by whatever means available, and try to locate the enemy in the Forest of Vernon. If there was no opposition, they were to move to the edge of the forest at Panilleuse and remain concealed until the battalion crossed over to join them.

Shortly after breakfast, the four jeeps slipped down into Vernon to join the mêlée on the waterfront. After much persuasion, they managed to get themselves ferried over the river in stormboats. On arrival in Vernonnet, they passed through the village and up the Gisors road, following the route taken by 'D' Company of the 4th Somersets earlier that morning. Just outside the built-up area they left the road, cautiously entering the dense forest by a narrow track.

Colonel Taylor was also party that morning to a ruse to confuse the enemy. Captain Anslow was told to take his carrier platoon and create a diversion downstream at Gaillon. With the aid of a 25-pounder field gun, a detachment of mortars and a section of carriers, his small force set out to simulate another crossing of the Seine. At around noon, the eastern bank of the river above Les Andelys was subjected to a bombardment of high explosive, smoke, mortar, machine-gun and rifle fire. The noise of this supposed attack resonated about the valley and hillside, no doubt adding to the enemy's feeling of insecurity.

Situation at 1200 Hours Saturday 26 August

It was now seventeen hours since the assault began. Only one of the 43rd Division's main objectives had been reached: Vernonnet had been captured.

General Thomas's problems were still growing: the bridge building had come to a halt; the close support rafts were only in intermittent use; all three spurs overlooking Vernon were still in enemy hands; three battalions were over the river, but none was more than 300 yards (274m) inland and the likelihood of having tanks across the river before dark, to stem any counter-attack, seemed remote.

Chapter 11

Afternoon, 26 August

At the headquarters of the German 49th Infantry Division in Beauvais, General Macholtz received the news of the crossing at Vernon with alarm. His division's left flank was already under pressure from the American crossings at Mantes, where the 18th German Air Force Division was fighting a losing battle in trying to contain the US Third Army's bridgehead over the Seine. Macholtz was expecting that at any moment the Americans would break out and drive down the valley on his side of the river. This threat, coupled with the news that Paris had fallen that day, left him unprepared for a new attack against his front mounted by the British 43rd Division. German intelligence had no idea that the British had reached the Seine. Was this a full-scale assault, or merely a diversionary raid? The general ordered an aerial reconnaissance to find out just what was happening at Vernon.

On the hill behind Vernon, in the area of St Marcel, the guns of the 179th Field Regiment RA were firing in support of the infantry across the river. Bombardier Sam Beard was acting Number One on one of the 25-pounder field guns. To shield his battery from any prying eyes, a huge camouflage net was stretched over the gun. Through its latticed ropework Beard could see the small shape of a friendly light aircraft buzzing around in the empty sky.

The Auster Mark IV aircraft above Vernon that morning was an air observation post from B Flight of 662 Squadron; its pilot was Captain Mohin. Mohin was spotting the fall of shot from the artillery on the ground and radioing back corrections to bring their fire on to target. Only three weeks before, he had had a very narrow escape when supporting the 43rd Division in an attack. A bullet had entered the cockpit and passed on up through the petrol tank above his head, missing his face by inches. In a few more minutes, he was not to be so fortunate.

At a much higher altitude, a Messerschmidt Bf 110 was heading for the same patch of sky. The German fighter was effecting the reconnaissance ordered by Macholtz to discover the British strength and intentions at the Seine. Armed with two 30mm cannon and four heavy machine-guns, the Messerschmidt was capable of over 300mph.

Inside the small cockpit of the Auster, Mohin could hear nothing above the noise of the plane's 130hp Lycoming engine. The roar of the Messerschmidt, as it swooped down from out of the sun, was lost to him. The kill was accomplished with one short, clinically efficient burst of cannon fire which tore the fabric-covered aircraft to shreds. The fury of the bombardment sent the Auster cartwheeling over and over towards the earth. Death came with a sickening ball of flame as the tiny plane hit the ground; a pall of black smoke billowing skywards to serve as brief memorial to its final flight.

The victor of the one-sided action continued down the river valley at high speed on its original mission. Once it had reached the end of the British positions, the Messerschmidt pulled up and, with a sweeping turn, came roaring back along the line of the river with all guns blazing, sending everyone ducking for cover. In reply, the anti-aircraft Bofors guns of the division opened up on the enemy aircraft.

Sam Beard was aware of the battle going on around him, but his gun kept to the task of supporting the infantry across the river. One of the Bofors was situated just a short way down the hill from his 25-pounder. As the German aircraft swept up the river valley, the anti-aircraft gun's detachment fired a stream of 40mm shells into the sky in an attempt to intercept the enemy plane. The gun's aimer was frantically trying to lock onto the swiftly moving Messerschmidt, his sole preoccupation being to keep the aircraft squarely in his sights. In doing so, the Bofors' long thin barrel swept low across the sky and the small shells began to pass dangerously close to the adjacent field gun on the higher ground. One errant projectile caught and snapped the tightly strained camouflage net just as the 25-pounder fired. The blast from the gun's muzzle set alight the net as it collapsed around Sam Beard and the rest of the crew. For a short while chaos reigned; men were rushing everywhere in their attempts to put out the fire, anxious lest the column of black smoke should act as a beacon to the marauding German aircraft. Fortunately, although the Messerschmidt returned and strafed the area, nobody was hurt.

By midday the situation at the water's edge showed little sign of improvement. The enemy still continued stubbornly to interfere with any movement along the river bank. Its presence on the high ground was keeping the few troops that were over the river contained in the vicinity of Vernonnet. This was now the perfect time for Macholtz to launch his counter-attack against the bridgehead. With the 43rd Division's intentions clearly revealed and with the high ground still controlled by the German 49th Division, a relatively small force, backed by tanks, could sweep the British back into the river.

General Thomas realised only too well what would happen if his lodgement was attacked with armour. To resist such a threat, he desperately needed tanks across the river as soon as possible, but the Bailey bridge stood no chance of being completed for at least another twenty-four hours. (Given that the work on the folding boat bridge had at that time ceased, even twenty-four hours seemed rather an optimistic assumption.) Thomas therefore decided that the engineers should build a tank raft to ferry some armour over. He suggested a site about a mile downstream from Vernon.

This new task added to the problems already facing the chief engineer, Brigadier Davey. There was a shortage, not in materials, as might be expected when considering just how far they were from the nearest supply dumps, but in manpower. Who was there available to build the rafts?

Brigadier Davey had no fewer than four Royal Engineers' formations under his command: 7th Army Troops Royal Engineers, 43rd Division Royal Engineers, XXX Corps Troops Royal Engineers and 15th (Kent) GHQ Troops Royal Engineers. Even so, he could not readily produce enough men for the job. The 7th Army Troops RE had travelled forward in Group 2 convoy and had arrived the previous night. They had been ordered down into Vernon where they now waited to begin their construction of the first Class 40 Bailey bridge. To use them on the tank raft would only serve to delay the commencement of this bridge. This was completely out of the question, for the construction of the Bailey was the single most important task of the whole operation. The bridge would carry over the Seine the reinforcements needed for the final expansion of the bridgehead and also the whole of XXX Corps, already closing inexorably on the river.

The 43rd Division's engineers were already fully occupied with the construction of the Class 9 folding boat bridge and its approaches.

XXX Corps' engineers were further back down the route in Pacy. They were still working round the clock to deal with the damaged road and rail bridges in the town. They were also totally exhausted and in no fit state to begin work on the complex task of raft-building.

This left the 15th (Kent) GHQ Troops Royal Engineers as the only group available to deal with the tank raft. In fact, as already mentioned, this unit had been especially trained on the rivers and lakes of Northern Ireland for an operation such as this, and was perfect for the job. Unfortunately, there was one big problem: most of the men were not at the Seine, but stranded some thirty miles short of the river, at Conches.

Lieutenant-Colonel Fayle's 15th GHQ Troops RE had been earmarked as the chief engineer's reserve. They were intended to build a Class 70 Bailey bridge later in the operation (this had by then been changed to a Class 40 Bailey). As such, they had been assigned road space in the less urgent Group 3 convoy for the move to Vernon. Two platoons of one field company (583 Field Company) had driven forward with the Assault Group and had provided crews for the stormboats during the attack. The few survivors of that ordeal were still recovering from the effects of the previous evening. Midday

Saturday 26 August found the remainder of the 15th's engineers immobile in a little French town, just when their special skills were desperately needed. The Royal Engineers, together with the RASC vehicles belonging to Group 3, had been halted in their advance eastwards by the Americans. This latter part of the Group 3 convoy had not made it across the start point, where the route crossed the US lines of communication, by the required time. As a result, they were shut out and the road closed to them whilst the Americans continued their withdrawal southwards.

It was a most frustrating time for Fayle; his highly trained sappers would be perfect for the raft-building. They were probably the most accomplished rafting formation in the whole of the army. However, since arriving in France, they had been employed on beach work and 'road-bashing'. The situation at the Seine would be an ideal proving ground for their special talents, but they were stranded some thirty miles away from the action whilst protocol demanded they keep off the roads reserved for the Americans. It all seemed too ridiculous to be true. Fayle sent word back for the 584 Field Company to burst their way through to the Seine; Lieutenant Tanner was to meet him in the square in Vernon at 1400 hours.

At his tactical HQ just short of Vernon, General Thomas pored over his maps. The proposed landing site for the tank rafts, on the far side of the river, was still overlooked by the enemy on top of the spur that the 4th Somersets were trying to clear. He was fearful of more delays being encountered and determined to keep up the pressure on the enemy. He therefore decided to consign the remainder of 214 Brigade over the river: Lieutenant-Colonel Taylor was ordered to take his 5th Duke of Cornwall's Light Infantry across in DUKWs to secure the rafting site, and Lieutenant-Colonel Nichol was told to get his 7th Somerset Light Infantry over the old road bridge and help seize the high spur and the forest beyond.

Piece by piece, Thomas was committing his infantry into the bottleneck that was the bridgehead, all the while expecting the inevitable German counter-attack.

Early afternoon saw some progress in clearing the other spur on the right-hand side of the bridgehead opposite Vernon. The two Wiltshire battalions were slowly flushing out the enemy from their hiding places.

On top of the cliffs, the men of 'A' Company of the 4th Wiltshires began beating their way through the thick undergrowth and woods. In places the way forward was barred by foliage so thick that the troops had to attack the dense vegetation with machetes. Progress slowed almost to a standstill. Nevertheless, the infantry's noisy passage did have the effect of warning the enemy of their approach and diverted their attention away from the river bank opposite to meet the new threat.

This respite in the harassing fire aimed at the British engineers encouraged work to restart on the folding boat bridge. More rafts were quickly brought upstream into position and the bridge at last began to take shape.

This happy state of affairs was not, however, allowed to continue for long. The German defenders soon realised just where their priorities lay and interdictory fire was resumed at every opportunity. Once more the brave sappers suffered in the exposed boats. Casualties quickly began to mount as the engineers pressed on resolutely, despite the constant interruptions.

At around 1400 hours, during one of the heaviest bouts of enemy fire, Thomas arrived at the waterfront with Brigadier Mole. They were both alarmed at the intensity of the resistance aimed at the unfortunate sappers out on the river. The losses could not be allowed to continue. In spite of the pressing need for the bridge to be brought quickly into service, Thomas could not afford the casualties being taken by his engineers. He ordered Evill to call his men off the river and stand down once again. They were to take cover until the cliffs opposite were completely cleared of the enemy. Things were continuing to look bleak.

Across the river, behind and to the right of Vernonnet, 'B' Company of the 1st Worcestershires had dug themselves in on either side of the road leading up the hill out of the village towards La Chapelle St Ouen. The enemy further along the lane were content to keep their distance. Major Algy Grubb had received orders from battalion HQ to remain where he was until relieved by the 5th Wiltshires. Events had quietened down somewhat and things were becoming 'boring'.

Grubb was fascinated by the scene unfolding across the valley from him. On the middle spur immediately behind Vernonnet, he could see the other two companies of the battalion moving up onto the high ground. These two companies should have been following him, had he gone the right way earlier in the day. As it was, he had a grandstand seat from which to watch the action. On the reverse slope of the hill he could see the German troops and lorries retiring out of sight of the British infantry advancing up the face. It amused Grubb to take long-range pot-shots at the retreating enemy, watching their startled faces through his field glasses.

A short way up the lane from where 'B' Company was hidden was a turning to the left that led to the village of Bois Jérôme. The enemy were concealed in the woods just beyond this junction. During the afternoon, Grubb's company was taken completely by surprise when six Germans on bicycles burst out of the side turning, heads down, pedalling furiously in single file towards Vernonnet. Their silent approach had caught 'B' Company off guard and the enemy were among the Worcestershires before anyone realised their presence. Gathering speed down the hill they might well have got away, but there was one man among the company who was on top of the situation. Corporal Chambers coolly brought his Bren gun to bear on the swiftly moving targets and opened fire. He killed them all; bicycles and bodies littered the road.

The startled men of 'B' Company jumped out of their slit trenches and pulled the debris out of sight. No sooner had they completed this task than they heard the sound of a vehicle approaching. This time they were ready.

A few moments later a lorry pulled out of the side road and into view. A Bren gun opened up at short range. Inside the lorry, the terrified driver slammed his foot to the floor and the truck roared forward. Accelerating swiftly, the wagon hurtled through the prone infantrymen. Soon, more guns opened up and everyone began having a pot-shot at the lorry. Bullets peppered the canvas sides, tearing them to shreds. Undaunted, the trapped driver realised his only hope of survival was to press on. Screeching from side to side, the lorry plunged on down the hill. Within seconds, it had disappeared from sight round a bend in the road.

Major Grubb could not believe his eyes. The truck had passed within feet of his company and yet had still managed to evade them. The memory of this spectacular escape still rankles in his thoughts even to this day, though for an entirely different reason:

> The lorry was immediately captured when it reached the village further down the road. It was subsequently found to contain a complete field photographic unit. Inside were numerous Leica cameras and other valuable equipment, none of which ever made it across the Seine; it all disappeared into kitbags as spoils of war. It was worth a fortune and we missed it all.

Situation at 1530 Hours Saturday 26 August
Over twenty hours had passed since the first assault and things were still behind schedule. In fact, the situation looked remarkably bleak for Thomas. In the last three hours, the only progress made by the division was to penetrate a few hundred yards further along the three spurs. Work on the bridge had ceased, there was no chance of tank rafts being ready before dawn and Thomas was now having to introduce his second brigade into the battle without the support of armour. If the German 49th Division counter-attacked the bridgehead now with tanks, all could be lost.

Chapter 12

Evening

By 1545 hours the bulk of the 5th Duke of Cornwall's Light Infantry had arrived in Vernon and arrangements were being made to ferry them over the river in DUKWs, in order to secure the proposed site for the tank raft. It was at about this time that the battalion HQ received a short radio message from its scout platoon across the river. The platoon reported that it had reached a set of cross tracks roughly in the centre of the Forest of Vernon, behind Vernonnet, and having met no opposition, was moving on to the edge of the forest. The vast woods appeared to be clear of the enemy. This was wonderful news and Lieutenant-Colonel Taylor rushed to inform his brigadier.

Taylor met Brigadier Essame talking with General Thomas on the main road just outside the town. He gave them both the good news, which coincidentally arrived at the same time as word came through of the completion of the mopping up, by the 4th Somersets, of the machine-gun nests and snipers on the cliffs to the left of Vernonnet. 'D' Company had turned the spur from the rear, capturing several anti-aircraft cannon dug in along a sunken road overlooking the river.

Thomas was delighted with the sudden turn of events. He decided to put the remainder of 214 Brigade across the river at once: the 7th Somerset Light Infantry were ordered to lead the way over the old road bridge and move into the Forest of Vernon, whilst the 5th DCLI were to follow closely behind, then move left down the river valley and occupy the village of Pressagny l'Orgueilleux just beyond the proposed tank ferry site. At last, his bridgehead was beginning to expand.

Across the Seine, on that long spur to the right of Vernonnet, the two Wiltshire battalions continued their noisy progress along the chalk cliffs and through the dense woods on the summit. The thick undergrowth had reduced the advance to a crawl. With three companies abreast, the 4th Wiltshires swept the face of the escarpment towards Giverny. Yet despite all the shouting and slashing at the almost impenetrable vegetation, the Wessexmen were still able to stumble upon a party of Germans playing cards! The startled group of enemy infantry was screened by a cordon of sentries. Both sides saw each other at the same moment and began blasting away with their guns. A ferocious little battle developed, which ended with the Germans retiring further into the woods, leaving several of their dead behind.

Along the face of the cliffs, the infantry came across many of the machine-gun posts that had caused such havoc with the attack the night before. Some had been knocked out by the tanks and artillery and at least one had been silenced by accurate fire from the machine-guns of the 8th Middlesex. They were deserted, but the troops carefully probed the empty dug-outs, ever cautious lest they should be booby-trapped.

Sergeant Butcher and his section from 'B' Company of the 4th Wiltshires were involved in clearing some of these posts overlooking Vernon. In total silence, they worked their way through the camouflaged gun sites. Suddenly, Butcher was jolted by the persistent ring of a muffled telephone bell. In vain, he searched for the noisy instrument, but found nothing. It was not until much later that he discovered that the offending ringing had come from a 'liberated' alarm clock in the pack of his corporal.

'D' Company, further in the woods, came close to several light self-propelled guns. This time, the enemy were well aware of their approach and opened fire. The attacking infantry were forced back by the small shells, which began to explode amongst the trees with deadly effect. Attempts to stalk the guns came to nothing. The vegetation was so thick that visibility was down to just a few yards. The enemy was determined to keep the British troops at arm's length and opened up with the troublesome shells at any sign of movement. Again and again, the Wiltshires tried to close on the cannon, but each attack was broken off as the shells homed in on any movement through the undergrowth.

Although these German guns were proving to be quite deadly to the troops clearing the spur, they were at least away from the front of the cliffs and were not interfering with activities across the water. Nevertheless, they still stubbornly refused to give in to 'D' Company and it was nearly dark before they decided to fall back to a prepared position, the rest of the battalion having by that time cleared the whole of the face of the cliffs opposite the crossing sites.

By the late afternoon, the Wiltshires had removed virtually all of the opposition capable of harassing the engineers engaged on the river. This enabled the divisional sappers to resume work on the Class 9 bridge. Without the interdictory fire from across the water, the 43rd's engineers were able to demonstrate their remarkable skills at bridge-building. In front of a gathering crowd of truly amazed French onlookers the bridge quickly took shape, but before it could be completed one more obstacle was placed in the path of the tired sappers.

The Germans were by this time in full knowledge of just what was going on at Vernon. To hinder the erection of any new bridges by the Allies, the enemy had blown a dam downstream, causing the water level to fall slowly, leaving an exposed stretch of slippery mud on each bank. Lieutenant-Colonel Tom Evill now found that he could not use a half-floating bay on the far side of his boat bridge because of the new water level. He therefore had to arrange for the bridge to terminate on a trestle. It wasn't a difficult engineering job, but nevertheless it added a few more precious minutes to the time taken for the construction. This done, the bridge was at last finished. At 1730 hours the first vehicle crossed over. The British had bridged the River Seine; DAVID was open for business.

Elsewhere in Vernon other Royal Engineers' formations were busy with the preliminary work for their own operations. At 1600 hours, the commander of 15th (Kent) GHQ Troops RE was waiting in the main square for the reconnaissance officer of his 584 Field Company.

Right on time, Lieutenant Tanner arrived to greet his CO with the news that the remainder of the party were still trying to cross the American lines of communication, but would probably be delayed for some time; the Americans would not allow the stranded British engineers across their route. It now seemed highly unlikely that Fayle would get these troops through to the Seine in time to complete the tank raft by the next morning, as General Thomas had ordered. Nevertheless, it was important that every effort was made to get the ferry in operation as soon as possible. Fayle was therefore given a party of the 43rd Division's engineers, 207 Field Park Company, to begin the preliminary work, even though it was realised that they would take much longer than his own trained specialists to complete the job. It was a start, but he knew that for the raft to have any chance of being ready before dawn he would have to have his own men there at Vernon. He instructed Lieutenant Tanner to get the rest of his party through to the river that evening, 'by hook or by crook'.

With the opening of the Class 9 bridge, the river banks could be given over to Lieutenant-Colonel Lloyd and his 7th Army Troops Royal Engineers to begin work on the first of the mighty Bailey bridges. Thomas did not want to risk this Bailey by starting it too soon and so the order to commence was delayed until everyone was quite sure. Then, at last, in the late afternoon, word was finally given for the work to start. After waiting patiently for so long, Lloyd's engineers thought that they had everything ready, but when they began to tackle the first task on the near bank – the infilling of a large bomb crater in line with the approaches – they discovered that someone had borrowed both the bulldozers to repair the damage to the road surface between Pacy and Vernon. It took until 1700 hours before two low-loaders had made the round trip to reclaim their property, by which time other work on the bridging site was well under way.

With both sides of the Seine now in friendly hands, and the far cliffs finally clear of the enemy, the construction of the Bailey could proceed just as it would have done on those countless exercises back in England. The plan was quite straightforward: one field company would build out from the near bank, another would be similarly employed on the far side, whilst a third field company would assemble the pontoons into piers and tow them into position. The line of the bridge was between the old demolished road bridge and the new Class 9 folding boat bridge (the original site, just downstream of the old bridge, had been abandoned as being too difficult).

Although this final position of the Bailey was not a perfect site for bridging operations, the few problems that existed were not insurmountable. The near bank was faced with masonry, which would have to be blasted away to give a gentle slope down to the water. The far side's landing point was covered with a huge pile of logs, which would have to be shifted to allow access. A small diversion from the far exit could temporarily link the bridge with the lane that led off the Class 9 bridge. This would at least enable it to carry traffic immediately after completion, until a new road could be forced through some back gardens to join the main road in Vernonnet. In fact, with so few major problems facing him, Tom Lloyd positively revelled in the thought of the whole operation:

> Stray shells were still dropping on the town, and each company in turn reported casualties, but there was no stonking, in the accepted meaning of the word, and on the whole it was good to be in Vernon that August day: the nicest little town we had seen in all our travels, with a fine, slow river just asking to be bridged.

With two field companies busily engaged in clearing both banks, the third company was sweeping its pontoon construction site for mines; none was found. (It is interesting to note that no mines were encountered anywhere during the battle of Vernon. The German collapse was too swift to allow an 'in-depth' defensive line to be constructed on the Seine, thus sparing the 43rd Division the agonies and delays of mine clearance.) The sappers then laid telegraph poles against the bank to allow the launching of the pontoons into the water and the site was ready for the bridging lorries.

From their harbouring place in the railway goods yard, the first of the 3-ton lorries carrying the pontoons made their way to the assembly area.

These vehicles were popularly known as 'four posters', for on each corner was a large pole that formed a cradle for the two pontoons on board, one on top of the other. Although made only of strong plywood, each pontoon weighed a ton. It took three pontoons to form a 60ft (18m) pier; two bow-shaped ends and a square box-like centre section. They were 6ft (1.8m) wide and 2 ft 6 in (0.7m) deep.

Watching his men from the bank, Tom Lloyd described the scene:

> The company had three cranes spaced along the river bank. As soon as a lorry had backed up alongside a crane a sapper clambered up onto the pontoons and fastened the crane sling to the upper one. The crane took the weight, and the lorry then shunted forward from under the pontoon, leaving it suspended, with the sapper still on board making sure that the bungs were in. The crane then swung the pontoon out, and lowered it onto the telegraph-pole launching ways, broadside on to the river. Other sappers fastened reins to it; the original one disconnected the crane sling, and then, clinging on to the hook, had himself swung up again onto the lorry, which by this time had shunted back into position, to repeat the process. Often he was hardly clear before the men holding the reins paid out, and let the pontoon go rushing down the ways in a crescendo that ended in an almighty splash – all to the accompaniment of much the same back-chat as would have been used by Shakespeare's soldiery on an evening such as this.

From those pontoons launched into the water the 'tripartite' piers were assembled and towed away downstream to the bridging site. On each bank, other lorries had deposited large piles of Bailey sections, and when the preparatory work on the approaches was finished work began on the bridge-building proper, although it was still to be some time before the Class 40 bridge (codenamed GOLIATH) took recognisable shape. To the 7th Army Troops RE, the process had been undertaken so many times before that it was second nature to them, but to many onlookers it was quite fascinating, as Lieutenant-Colonel Lloyd recounts:

> Fitting the Bailey together, and putting it on pontoons, hardly bears detailed description, although it had been known to interest the most unlikely people. There was the old lady who, when we were training back in the UK, used to bring her knitting and watch, and was one day overheard holding her grandchildren spellbound with: 'And now, my dears, you see how after they have slipped the transoms through, they put

the rakers in, and then the swaybraces, and they don't tighten up the transom clamps until last of all.'

Likewise in Vernon, civilian spectators were fascinated by all the bustling activity needed to construct a pontoon bridge. Jacques Cambuza visited the building site in the early evening. He was confronted with a scene the like of which he doesn't think he will ever see again:

Everywhere there was intense activity. It was miraculous to witness the orderly manner in which the English soldiers worked to build the bridges. Firstly, they had to demolish one of the two very superior residences which were on the main street close to the Pont de Vernon. Then they pulled down a house that had been burned by the Germans a few days previously. They moved hundreds of cubic metres of earth in order to make a smooth descent towards the bank of the Seine. All the while perfect order reigned: some heaved materials around, others in lorries brought up steel plates from a depot back in the town. Everything seemed worked out to an exact plan. As a bulldozer lifted up building materials, the soldiers, one metre in front of the machine, would drop back in perfect discipline. Not a moment was wasted. Out on the river, pontoons were manoeuvred into position by small boats powered by independent engines. With the light beginning to fade, girders were thrown from one pontoon to another and the bridges were built before my very eyes.

By nightfall the bridge had taken clear shape. Lloyd was pleased with the progress that his formation had made, but realised that in the gathering darkness, pierced only by a pale blue glow from the heavily shaded bridging lights, things would be more difficult. He left his two companies on each bank to work on, but reduced their strength so that the majority would be fresh in the morning. Then, around midnight, Lloyd stood his third company down. By that time they had managed to launch ninety pontoons, sufficient for any immediate needs; he would thereby 'Save them from the worry and tedium of struggling to do in the dark what could be done in daylight in a fraction of the time.'

In the late afternoon, as the divisional engineers were working feverishly to complete the final phase of the Class 9 bridge, the remaining two battalions of 214 Brigade began their passage across the river. The 7th Somerset Light Infantry took the lead in a long line of infantry that rose up and down over the switchback remains of the old Pont de Vernon. Their arrival on the far side in Vernonnet was greeted with wild enthusiasm by the

Troops of the 43rd Division arrive in Vernon and immediately make friends with local children by handing out sweets. (*Imperial War Museum*)

The blown railway bridge at Vernon downstream of the road bridge. (*Ken Ford*)

Aerial photograph of Vernon taken on 14 August and used in the planning of Operation Neptune. (*Crown Copyright*)

The hurriedly built Bailey bridge at Pacy ten miles short of Vernon, which proved to be vital during the dash to the Seine. (*Imperial War Museum*)

Major General G. Ivor Thomas, Commander 43rd (Wessex) Division. (*Pat Spencer Moore*)

Infantry of the 4th Wiltshires take a rest from their task of guarding the town not long after arriving in Vernon. (*Imperial War Museum*)

Carrying parties from the 4th Wiltshires struggle down to the river with an assault boat. (*Imperial War Museum*)

The first waves of the 5th Wiltshires' attack. Within the next few minutes most of these men would be dead. (*Imperial War Museum*)

Troops from No. 8 Platoon from A Company of the 5th Wiltshires disappear into the smoke on their fateful assault. (*Imperial War Museum*)

Men of the 1st Worcestershires file down to the river before their crossing. (*Imperial War Museum*)

Infantry negotiate the steep steps that led onto the ruins of the old road bridge. As each man reached the top, he was exposed in silhouette to any German sniper covering the bridge. (*Imperial War Museum*)

The building in Vernonnet which housed the machine-gun post that covered the German end of the road bridge. It was this gun which caused the 1st Worcestershires so much trouble during their first attempt at crossing the Seine. (*Ken Ford*)

A Cromwell tank of the 15th/19th Kings Royal Hussars firing in support of the crossings. (*Imperial War Museum*)

Royal Engineers build a Class 9 raft on a section of the river shielded from the enemy by a smokescreen. (*Imperial War Museum*)

The road on the far side of the Seine looking towards Giverny. The white house on the left was the HQ of A Company, 5th Wiltshires. Major Milne's position was overlooked by the German-held cliffs behind. The grassy meadows on the right lead down to the Seine. (*Ken Ford*)

Major A.A. 'Algy' Grubb of the 1st Worcestershire Regiment. (*Ken Ford*)

DUKWs ferrying supplies over the Seine, photographed from the old road bridge. (*Imperial War Museum*)

The 4th Dorsets cross the newly opened Class 9 bridge. Work on the first Bailey bridge continues in the background. (*Imperial War Museum*)

Royal Engineers begin preparatory work on the first Bailey bridge. The crossing place for the 5th Wiltshires' assault is in the background. (*Imperial War Museum*)

Lieutenant Michael Trasenster of the 4th/7th Dragoon Guards commanded the first tank, *Winchester*, across the Seine. (*M. Trasenster*)

German prisoners and a French civilian move back across the boat bridge. (*Imperial War Museum*)

Tiger tank knocked out by the 6-pounder guns of the 1st Worcestershires on the Gisors road. (*Ken Ford*)

Follow-up troops file across the switchback remains of the old road bridge. The DUKW landing site is visible in the left background. (*Imperial War Museum*)

Royal Engineers prepare a new length of Class 9 boat bridge to replace a section damaged by enemy shell fire. (*Imperial War Museum*)

Sergeant Tucker RE watches 130 Brigade crossing the river via the boat bridge. The first Bailey bridge in the background nears completion. (*Imperial War Museum*)

Follow-up troops move inland into the Wessex Division's bridgehead. (*Imperial War Museum*)

A Sherman Firefly tank of the 4th/7th Dragoon Guards crosses the Seine ready to deal with enemy counter-attacks. (*Imperial War Museum*)

'A Nos Liberateurs': the memorial to the men of the 5th Wiltshires killed in the battle to take La Chapelle St Ouen. (*Ken Ford*)

The drive across northern France begins. Tanks of the British Second Army cross the River Seine at Vernon into the lodgement won by the 43rd Division. (*Imperial War Museum*)

Field Marshal Montgomery crosses the River Seine at Vernon. (*Imperial War Museum*)

local populace. The battle had by that time moved on out of the village and its inhabitants were anxious to meet their liberators. Excited groups of French civilians lined the roads, pressing gifts into the hands of the marching soldiers: flowers, fruit and, much to the alarm of the officers, cider and wine. The Somersets marched on through the streets towards the positions up on the high ground held by their sister battalion, the 4th, then moved on into the dark interior of the Forest of Vernon.

Since arriving in France, all the fighting endured by the division had been among the fields and meadows of the Normandy countryside. On the exposed slopes of Hill 112 and Mont Pinçon, the infantry had used their picks and shovels to get below ground as quickly as possible. Shelter from the view of the enemy was everything; their very survival depended on it. Now, here in the deep forest, there was an abundance of cover, but its presence was not at all reassuring. For the first time, the battalion was enveloped in dense woods, preparing itself for an unfamiliar type of warfare. The surroundings were like the dark woods of childhood nightmares, each bush and tree hiding something quite terrible.

The forest was traversed by a few narrow rides, with occasional clearings deep with bracken. Visibility, once off the tracks, was very limited; movement only twenty yards away from the small pathways was swallowed up in the gloom of the thick woods. With daylight beginning to fade in the early evening, Lieutenant-Colonel Nichol decided not to risk his battalion in the gathering darkness and set out his four companies in a tight diamond formation across the main ride through the forest. If the enemy came at them during the night, they would be ready.

Following closely behind the Somersets over the old bridge was Taylor with his 5th DCLI. They also received the same tumultuous welcome in Vernonnet. For a moment the festivities threatened to disrupt the battalion's orderly progress through the village, but the column kept steadily moving forward in spite of all the distractions. It marched on down the road to Pressagny l'Orgueilleux towards the tank ferry site, until it reached the base of the spur overlooking the river. 'B' Company was sent up onto the high ground to act as a moving flank guard, whilst the main body continued along the road parallel to the river.

The two-mile journey to Pressagny passed without incident. Arriving just outside the village in the early evening, Taylor decided to call a halt there. He was concerned about the welcome his battalion might receive from the local inhabitants and also about the effects any home-brewed cider or calvados might have on his men.

As a result of the heavy casualties the battalion had taken in the earlier fighting, the 5th DCLI contained only three companies. Colonel Taylor set his troops to cover this left flank of the division's bridgehead. The village of Pressagny l'Orgueilleux lies only a hundred yards (91m) from the northern edge of the Forest of Vernon. At the entrance to the village is a large Calvary. Taylor placed a company on each side of this wayside crucifix, about fifty yards (45m) short of any houses. His third company was positioned around 500 yards (456m) back towards Vernonnet, just inside the forest, blocking some cross tracks.

Battalion HQ was located in le Château de la Madeleine, a large house by the side of the main road leading to the village. The château was in use as a home for orphan boys, run by a monk dressed in a long brown habit and sporting a bushy beard. Brother André put on a fine show of hospitality for the Cornishmen, making them feel most welcome.

The lightning advance to the Seine, coupled with the rapturous welcome given to the battalion and the absence of any sight of the enemy, led to a

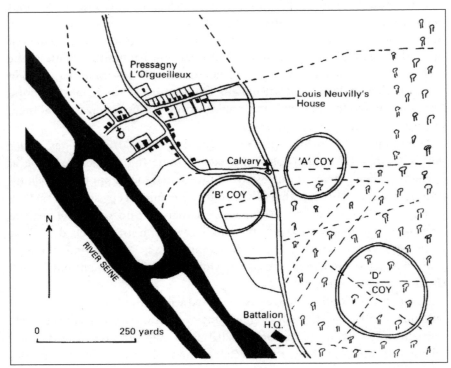

Map 7. 5th Duke of Cornwall's Light Infantry in Pressagny l'Orgueilleux on Saturday evening, 26 August.

feeling within the unit that the German army was finished in France. Its headlong retreat meant that danger was past. Colonel Taylor recalls:

> There was a great euphoria at that time, which was general to the British Second Army, and was later reflected in the attitude in the Arnhem battles to some extent, for, having advanced all that way since defeating the Germans in Normandy, one felt that the war had not long to run. Later that night as we were having supper, my intelligence officer David Willcocks asked, 'What about the blackout, sir?' to which I replied, 'To hell with the blackout, the war is almost over.' Rather a stupid remark on my part I'm afraid, as later events were to prove.

Situation at 1900 Hours Saturday 26 August

In a relatively short space of time the situation on the bridgehead had rapidly improved. Twenty-four hours after the initial assault, Thomas had two brigades across the river and a Class 9 bridge open to speed more men and vehicles into the lodgement area. By the next morning, he planned to have the Class 40 raft ferrying tanks over to strengthen his hold on the bridgehead. Prospects looked bright for the completion of the Bailey by the next evening and, with its opening, a stream of armour and guns could pour across the river. For the first time since the start of the crossing, Thomas felt that he was in total command of the bridgehead. Although it was only three miles long and barely a mile deep, his six battalions firmly controlled the area. The expected enemy counter-attack had not materialised and, since the assault, resistance had been spasmodic and defensive. Thomas felt it reasonable to assume that the enemy was still retreating across northern France. Both brigades were ordered to dig in for the night and be ready to resume the advance inland as soon as possible after first light.

In fact the German 49th Division was still there, close by. General Macholtz had received details of the aerial reconnaissance and had ordered a counter-attack to be made immediately. However, these orders were delayed, arriving far too late for a concerted effort to be carried out that evening. And so, whilst the Wessexmen spent a quiet night in their hastily dug slit trenches, it was the enemy's turn to gather silently for the attack.

Chapter 13

The Second Night

The evening of 26 August was cloudy, with a stiffening breeze. As the night began to close in, the sky looked heavy with rain. Four miles outside Vernon, on the long straight road that leads to Pacy-sur-Eure, Lieutenant Tanner paced impatiently up and down in the gathering darkness. He was beginning to get worried by the non-arrival of his men. 'What can be holding them up?' he thought. 'Will they never come?' and, more alarmingly, 'What shall I do if they don't come at all?' The one-and-a-half platoons of 584 Field Company Royal Engineers were long overdue. It was looking increasingly unlikely that the tank ferry would be completed before dawn.

At about 2100 hours, much to the relief of Lieutenant Tanner, the familiar sight of the trucks and half-tracks belonging to the rest of the company came tearing along the road towards him. They had managed to talk their way through the American checkpoint, although it had been a most frustrating and tedious exercise. Vital hours had been wasted and Tanner quickly urged them on down to the river. There was no time for a post-mortem. The 15th (Kent) GHQ Troops RE at last had their rafting experts on the Seine.

The village of Pressagny l'Orgueilleux nestles along the east bank of the River Seine, stretched out on either side of the road that runs down the right-hand side of the river valley. It then comprised just one long street, with several small lanes branching off, leading to a few farm buildings. A short way from the village square one such lane, Rue de la Marette, leads eastwards through the Forest of Vernon towards the village of Panilleuse. Along this road, set back behind a small courtyard, stood the home of a Monsieur Neuvilly.

Louis Neuvilly was the leader of the resistance in the village. A 36-year-old forestry worker, he and his pretty wife Jermaine had spent most of the war in active opposition to the German occupation. Neuvilly was an old soldier, a veteran of the early struggle against the Bosche. During the German invasion of 1940 he had fought in Belgium and France with his regiment, the Sixième Groupe de Reconnaissance de Corps d'Armée and was evacuated with the British at Dunkirk. Nonetheless, his war was far from over, for he soon re-embarked for France and the fighting, this time in the

Loire valley. After France had capitulated, he was demobilised and returned to his home at Pressagny l'Orgueilleux in August 1940.

Once normality had returned to his village, he set about organising a resistance group with three other friends. He was told that his cell had to be six strong to join the organised resistance movement in the area, so he recruited two more men and joined the 'Vengeances' group, led in Vernon by Madame Marcelle Fournier.

The next two years saw Neuvilly and his men carrying out acts of sabotage in the locality against German communications and river traffic. He was in charge of an arms dump, buried in the woods, made up of weapons that had been left by the retreating French troops in 1940. Later he kept a supply of explosives for use by other groups. His life was fraught with danger, not only from the Germans, but even from his own countrymen. Twice he was denounced by other villagers but both times evaded arrest. On one occasion, the police arrived unannounced to search his house. He had, in fact, several guns in the building, but they were buried in his loft under a 'mud pat' made only two days previously by his wife and they were never found. Another time, just eleven days before the British arrived, Neuvilly had been denounced once again, this time by a different villager, who happened to have a German wife. On this occasion, it was Neuvilly who took action, confronting the couple with their treachery. There was a struggle in which he was shot in the hand, but it was the two collaborators who were the ultimate losers; they were killed and their bodies dumped in the Seine. In June 1944, Louis Neuvilly was made 'sergent chef' FFI.

On the evening of 26 August, the long-awaited liberation looked set to happen. Neuvilly had spent the previous twenty-four hours sending news back across the river to the FFI, giving details of the German movements between Pressagny and Panilleuse. At around 1900 hours, a messenger told him of the DCLI's arrival on the outskirts of the village, explaining that the English troops had halted there and were digging in on either side of the Calvary. Neuvilly knew that there was a party of Germans quite close by in the woods near the next village of Panilleuse and was anxious to give the news to the British. He could not, unfortunately, speak any English. However, in the next village there was a doctor called Soulier, who could speak perfect English. The doctor was also a member of the resistance. Neuvilly sent his young wife to fetch the man.

The lane from Pressagny l'Orgueilleux to Panilleuse passes through the dark Forest of Vernon and then on across open fields before dropping down between two farms into the village. As Madame Neuvilly cycled along in the warm evening air, shells began to fall around her. The British field guns miles back on the other side of the river were trying to 'home in' on the German artillery known to be nearby. Just before she reached Panilleuse, she was stopped by a German patrol. The enemy soldiers demanded to know what she was doing. She told them that she was getting milk from the farm for her young children, pointing to a milk pail hanging on the handlebars of her bicycle. At first they were suspicious, but when she began to get agitated and tearful, saying she was worried for her children's safety, they relented and let her pass. Docteur Soulier was collected and brought back to Pressagny to act as an interpreter.

By late evening, the 5th Duke of Cornwall's Light Infantry had completed their digging in and were watching for any movement coming from the direction of the village. Everything seemed quiet and peaceful, so much so that many of the infantry had settled down for the night. A patrol was sent into the village, accompanied by the forward observation officer from the 179th Field Regiment Royal Artillery, to gather information about the enemy. The gunner officer in his scout carrier motored into the small square and asked if there were any FFI present in Pressagny. Indeed there were; Monsieur Neuvilly was quickly sent for.

It was the moment that Louis Neuvilly had long been waiting for; the liberation of his village was at hand. Both he and his wife reverently pulled on their FFI armbands, emblazoned with the Cross of Lorraine, that showed them to be patriotic soldiers of France. Then he left his wife Jermaine with the doctor and proudly marched down the road to the village square to greet the English captain.

Details of the German presence near the village were given and Neuvilly offered to show the British officer where the enemy were to be found. He beckoned for the officer to follow him to the edge of the village. Together, they walked towards the lane where this 'sergent chef' of the FFI had his home. Disaster was only a few steps away, for as they rounded the corner into the Rue de la Marette, they came face to face with two Germans only feet in front of them.

Neuvilly was the first to react: he threw himself bodily across the two enemy soldiers just as the first German raised his weapon. A long sustained burst of machine-gun fire hit the Frenchman and he slumped to the ground. The captain, armed only with a pistol, ducked back around the corner as bullets began ricocheting around him off the solid stone walls lining the street, killing a young French lad standing just outside a house. The two Germans had been equally surprised by the sudden confrontation and turned around to run back down the narrow lane towards their own positions. Neuvilly lay motionless in a rapidly growing pool of blood. He had been shot over twenty times.

Both the English captain and other French FFI men soon returned with aid for the unfortunate Neuvilly. Miraculously he was still alive, though horribly wounded. They picked up his blood-covered body and rushed it back to battalion HQ in le Château de la Madeleine. Morphine was pumped into his body to relieve the pain as he regained consciousness. Lying there on a stretcher beside the château, he recognised the bearded figure of Brother André, head of the boys' school. Neuvilly knew this man to be a collaborator with the Germans and denounced him forcefully to the British soldiers. (It was quite true, the monk was arrested and later confessed.)

Within minutes, Neuvilly was taken by ambulance to an advance dressing station near Vernonnet. After emergency treatment, he was transferred to a field hospital near Pacy, where he was operated on. Within hours he was on his way back down the lines to an airfield outside Bayeux, where he boarded a plane and was immediately flown to Bristol. He was to spend the next ten months in hospital in Newport (officially given the rank of corporal in the British army) before he was eventually shipped back to France. Once there, he was to spend still more time in hospital in Paris before he was well enough to return to his home two months later. For his bravery, Monsieur Louis Neuvilly was awarded the King's Medal for Courage.

With the Cornwalls now aware that there was a German presence in or around Pressagny, Lieutenant-Colonel Taylor ordered patrols to be stepped up throughout the night. Nothing more was seen or heard until, in the early hours of the morning, Taylor was awakened by tracer fire slapping past the window of his battalion HQ and a garbled message was received claiming that 'B' Company had been overrun. The Cornishmen had been taken completely by surprise. A patrol from 'B' Company had been returning through the village in the pouring rain when, whether by design or accident, a German patrol had attached itself to their rear. Major Hingston was the first to notice something was amiss. As he waited on the road for his men to approach the lines, he saw some shadowy figures moving behind the patrol. He challenged the enemy who replied immediately with a burst of fire and rushed forward. At this crucial moment the Bren gun covering the road jammed. Within seconds the enemy were among the British infantry. Utter confusion reigned; it was impossible to tell friend from foe in the darkness. Everyone fired at anything that moved. For the Germans, it was difficult to locate the British in their slit trenches and they, too, lay flat against the earth. The brief struggle ended as the German troops silently withdrew back into the village.

Behind, and to the right of 'B' Company, 'A' Company heard these sounds of battle with alarm. Now rudely awakened from their peaceful rest, the troops stood to and peered into the black, rainy night. Nothing could be seen on their front, but they did hear the noise of a tracked vehicle approaching. To their great relief, it did not sound heavy enough to be a tank and the offending machine halted on the road well in front of their positions. Even so, it did not tempt the Cornishmen from their trenches, nor did they reveal their presence to the enemy. They waited in silence, alerted to the fact that not all the units of the German army were engaged in headlong retreat as was generally believed, but some were about to try to regain the ground that had been lost to the British bridgehead.

The first real counter-attack directed at the 43rd Division's crossings was launched by the German 49th Division against the 5th DCLI just before dawn on 27 August and achieved almost total surprise. Aided by an early morning mist after the night's heavy rain, two companies from the German 148 Regiment crept through the cornfields and rushed an exposed platoon of 'B' Company, holding the road junction near the Calvary. The platoon was quickly swamped, easily overrun by the superior numbers of German infantry. Frightened survivors fell back on 'A' Company, whilst the enemy pushed on through the gap with guns blazing, throwing grenades as they went. Within minutes, the Germans were behind both British companies. Some continued down the road towards the battalion HQ, whilst others gathered in a small hollow between the three platoons of 'A' Company and the forest. It came as a great shock for the Wessexmen to be overwhelmed in so short a space of time.

Both sides had become inextricably mixed in the dark and there followed a deadly game of hide-and-seek as each side sought to gain advantage over the other. Crouched in their slit trenches, the English opened up with rifle and Bren-gun fire at the shadowy figures, receiving stick grenades in reply. Company Sergeant-Major Philp fired a burst of Bren into the enemy at very close range, knocking out four or five of them. He also shot up a machine-gun team which had set up its weapon only ten yards from his trench. The situation remained precarious for the Cornwalls, with the enemy ensconced virtually on top of them. There was no longer any front or rear to the Wessexmen's positions: the enemy were all around. Major Parker decided to take drastic action to ease his dilemma.

By whispered words of command, he passed orders for his men to hold their fire. In the silence, he used the telephone to contact Colonel Taylor at battalion HQ, explaining his serious situation to his commander. Taylor had by this time turned out all the headquarters staff to man their battle positions and had sent the scout platoon to give support to his surrounded companies. Major Parker then made a desperate decision and requested that artillery fire be brought down on his company's positions. Taylor agreed to this alarming proposal, trusting to the efficiency of the infantry's slit trenches to protect them.

To be under shell fire, crouched in a narrow dug-out with only earth for protection was, for any man, a terrifying experience. The Cornwalls were now being asked to endure another artillery barrage, fired not by the Germans but by their own comrades a few miles back across the river; British shells intended for the enemy, but heading straight for their shallow trenches. It was a brave decision on the part of Major Parker.

The very first salvoes landed right on target; the earth erupted all around 'A' Company's trenches, throwing the startled Germans into utter confusion. The Cornwalls meanwhile cowered low in their holes, pressing themselves into the dirt, praying to God to be spared a direct hit. For the enemy, there was no shelter. They quickly took flight; some disappearing into the forest, while others scattered down the road towards Vernonnet where they ran into more trouble from the battalion HQ defence. Then they, too, ducked into the woods to seek refuge. During this bombardment, 'A' Company received only three casualties from the shelling, but two prisoners, taken by the fleeing enemy, were later found dead, having been murdered in cold blood.

With the routed enemy moving eastwards into the Forest of Vernon, it was now 'D' Company's turn to face an attack, coming, not as they had expected and planned for, from the front, but from their supposedly safe rear. This third company of the 5th Duke of Cornwall's was deployed around a set of cross tracks in the forest, just a few hundred yards from the battalion command post in the château, guarding the approach through the woods. The retreating German rabble now ran headlong into their rear, immediately coming up against one isolated section post. A bloody little battle quickly followed. This small detachment of the Cornwalls put up a spirited resistance against superior odds, but were eventually overwhelmed by the two enemy companies swarming through the thick woods. They fought on to the end, inflicting losses on the enemy, but it was soon over. The section was annihilated; every man in the post was killed.

For a short while there was utter confusion in 'D' Company. Frightened stragglers fell back on the battalion HQ as once again the British infantry was split wide open by the German incursions into their lines. However, instead of exploiting the situation, the enemy simply carried on with their retreat and disappeared further into the forest, leaving almost as swiftly as they had arrived.

The whole action had lasted about twenty minutes and the 5th Duke of Cornwall's Light Infantry could count themselves lucky to have escaped so lightly. In the darkness, the enemy had passed completely through their lines to within yards of their battalion headquarters. If the German attack had been pushed home with a little more determination, it could well have been disastrous for the whole bridgehead. As it was, apart from a relatively small number of casualties, nothing was lost. The Cornwalls still held the road to Vernonnet and the area covering the tank ferry site and, with dawn beginning to light up the eastern sky, help would soon be on its way in the shape of tanks, just as soon as the Class 40 raft opened up.

The Cromwell tanks from 'C' Squadron of the King's Royal Hussars had spent most of Saturday in Vernon, firing in support of the infantry across the river. As the tide of battle ebbed inland from the face of the cliffs opposite, the squadron was withdrawn to harbour on top of the hill to the west of the town. The tank crews had been in continuous action, closed up in their tanks, all day long. Although dead tired, the first job always, when pulled out of the line, was to replenish ammunition stocks and make each tank ready once again for action. By the time this was completed, the crews felt ready for some rest and a meal. Unfortunately, to add to their discomfort, it began to rain. They had had no opportunity to prepare a hot meal or drink all day and the downpour hampered their cooking arrangements. It was a frustrated squadron that bedded down for the night to await the completion of the Bailey bridge the next day and with it, its means of passage over the River Seine.

The crews were in for a rude surprise, for no sooner had they become settled than a message was received ordering the squadron to cross the river on a tank raft that was at that very moment in the course of construction, just a mile downstream from Vernon. The squadron was told to alternate troop by troop with the 4th/7th Royal Dragoon Guards and support 129 Brigade in their advance the next day. All tank commanders were to reconnoitre the crossing places immediately, with the first tanks expected to cross around midnight. It was the start of a long and frustrating night for the tank crews of the Hussars.

Between the villages of Pressagny l'Orgueilleux, held by the Cornwalls, and Vernonnet was a stretch of river that became the scene of furious activity during the night, as the sappers from the 15th (Kent) GHQ Troops RE struggled to get the tank ferry into operation before morning. The falling water level, a direct result of the German demolition of the dam downstream at Gaillon, was causing difficulties.

The original site on the far bank, suggested by General Thomas, proved to be unsatisfactory for it had turned out to be another island. An alternative site was found a little further downstream, but it did mean that the round trip for the tank raft would now be almost half a mile. It was not the most desirable of landing places, but it was the best available. A reconnaissance had shown there to be few possible exits because of the exceptionally low level of the water and the soft mud on the banks. Nevertheless, Colonel Fayle and his engineers set to their task despite the darkness, mud, rain and problems on the far side. All caution was abandoned as headlights from the trucks illuminated the scene and the sappers worked without stop to make up for lost time. There were no reprisals from the enemy; although a few derisory shells arrived from time to time during the night, they caused no harm. Ironically, there were some Germans quite close by to all this activity, for around dawn some friendly infantry on the far side evicted a party of the enemy from a cottage overlooking the ferry site. They had apparently been there all night, but chose not to interfere with the operations, being of rather low morale. By 0600 hours, the Class 40 raft was complete and almost ready for use.

The first vehicle across was a bulldozer needed to clear the approaches. All went well with this maiden load until the great earthmover attempted to pull away from the ferry; it became stuck fast in the oozing mud, blocking the hastily constructed ramp. The situation was hopeless, the bulldozer would not move. Fayle decided to change the landing place once again to a new site further downstream alongside a beached river barge. Inevitably, there were more delays and this added to the discomfort of the tank crews, who had been waiting close by for several hours. Ever since midnight, they had been expecting to be called down to the raft and were very tired. Then, at last, word arrived that the ferry was ready for use.

A battle-scarred 75mm Sherman tank clattered down the ramp and on to the raft. Tank No 27 of 'A' Squadron 4th/7th Royal Dragoon Guards was commanded by Lieutenant Michael Trasenster. He was a Hampshire man and had named his tank *Winchester* after the county town and after his old school. Trasenster had landed in *Winchester* on D-Day, going on to fight through the proving grounds of the Normandy battlefields. The tank was now to have the distinction of being the first British armour across the Seine. It was, nevertheless, a distinction that its commander felt he could well do without after seeing the size of the river and hearing how the crossing was to be made.

Trasenster had returned to his regiment just a few days previously from a demolition course. It was normal after an absence such as this or through leave, to be given a roughish kind of job on rejoining the squadron. He was therefore hardly surprised when his squadron commander, Major Jackie Goldsmid, told him that his troop was to take the lead for the Seine crossing, the first tank to go over being *Winchester*.

The previous night's rain had stopped, leaving the air still and fresh; a slight mist lay low on the water. The day once again looked as though it would be bright and sunny. The ferry consisted of a length of Bailey, resting on two rafts each made up of three box sections. On each corner of these two tripartite piers was an outboard motor which coughed noisily into life as soon as the tank came on board. Crouching alongside each of these power units was a sapper, his eyes fixed on the raft's commander, watching intently for the helm orders. Every signal was prefaced by a blast on the officer's whistle and so, just as they had done in all the countless trial runs on the rivers and lakes of Northern Ireland, the 15th (Kent) GHQ Troops RE brought the huge unwieldy craft smoothly out into mid-river, sliding slowly downstream towards the hastily prepared new landing site.

The area on the far bank was thick with mud. The falling water level had left a wide bank of soft ground to be traversed before reaching the grassy banks. As the raft touched the opposite shore, *Winchester* edged its way down the ramp and slithered deep into the mire, in more ways than one, for the tank became stuck fast. The Sherman's great flailing tracks and roaring engine served only to carve a deep rut in the oozing sludge. Lieutenant Trasenster and his trailblazing Sherman had come to an abrupt halt.

The engineers on the raft looked down helplessly at the stranded monster, but there was nothing they could do to help. Their task was complete, and a shrill blast on the whistle soon set the raft in motion for the return journey back to the friendly shore. Trasenster jumped down from the turret and watched as the ferry faded from sight on the misty river; he and his tank were alone.

A stranded tank, whilst not completely impotent – it does after all still have its main armament available – nevertheless lacks a certain manoeuvrability and it was this manoeuvrability that was always one of the Sherman's greatest assets. The Allied tanks were never a match for the bigger German Tigers and Panthers but they used their relative agility to good effect, especially when attempting to evade the enemy's lethal intentions. There should have been friendly troops nearby, but none was to be seen. To add to Trasenster's feeling of insecurity, just a few hundred yards inland were the high, tree-covered cliffs that seemed to overlook his every move.

Not wishing to dwell on what might or might not be about to happen, the tank commander set off along the river bank to look for a more suitable landing site for the next tank to cross. A short distance downstream he found an area that appeared more promising. The bank was slightly lower, with a gentle run up to the firm ground; he decided to direct the ferry to land there. The other tank in his troop was commanded by Sergeant Reg Cox, an old crew member of his. Cox had landed with Trasenster on D-Day and had fought with him in Normandy before he was given command of his own tank. Once Cox had landed, this second tank could be brought upstream to help extricate the troop commander's bogged-down Sherman.

Now feeling a little happier about his imminent rescue, Trasenster thought he would have a look at the stranded river barge, beached near his tank. The craft, one of the many that littered this stretch of river, had been damaged by air attack, most likely from Allied fighter-bombers that had strafed all river traffic over the previous weeks in an effort to prevent enemy movement on the Seine. Still flying from its bow was a pennant, the name *Elan* picked out in gold on a blue background. Trasenster removed this flag and took it as a souvenir.

Back in Pressagny l'Orgueilleux, Colonel George Taylor was reflecting on the happenings earlier that morning. Twice his line had been penetrated by the enemy, although both times the position had been saved. He was concerned that a concerted attack against this left flank of the bridgehead, if successful, would leave the tank ferry, and indeed the whole lodgement area, wide open. He decided to stiffen the resolve of his men by issuing a Special Order of the Day. In it, he stressed to his battalion the importance of holding the left flank and ordered them that '... this position WILL be held TO THE LAST MAN AND THE LAST ROUND'. The 5th Duke of Cornwall's Light Infantry would not be moved.

Situation at 0600 Hours Sunday 27 August
During the previous evening and all through that night, traffic had been flowing across the Class 9 folding boat bridge from Vernon to Vernonnet. The two brigades which were already over the river had been reinforced by their transport and headquarters and, more importantly, anti-tank guns. Towards daybreak, armoured cars of the division's reconnaissance regiment crossed over, to move inland and join the infantry. Slowly the bridgehead began to fill with the bulk of the division. Soon there would be tanks across to help consolidate the gains made by the infantry the day before. The lodgement was at last beginning to look fairly secure. If a counter-attack was to come, although the prevailing feeling was that the enemy had pulled out, then Thomas felt he was ready. He ordered all the battalions in the bridgehead to advance inland at first light.

Chapter 14

Advance Inland

The attack against the 5th Duke of Cornwall's Light Infantry during the early hours of the morning had left the brigade commander, Brigadier Hubert Essame, anxious for the security of the rafting site covered by the battalion. To increase the Cornwalls' firepower, Essame sent several armoured cars from the 43rd Reconnaissance Regiment up to Taylor and his men, just as soon as the vehicles had crossed over the light bridge from Vernon. They were a very welcome addition to the three depleted companies holding this exposed flank. In view of the importance of Pressagny and the ferry site, he also ordered that the first troop of tanks ferried over the river should also go to Taylor's assistance. He had originally intended that these tanks should go to help strengthen the remainder of his brigade on their advance inland, but felt that the threat to the left flank had created a greater need.

Brigadier Essame now turned his attention to his other two battalions: the 1st Worcestershires and the 7th Somerset Light Infantry. The 1st Worcestershires had recently rejoined 214 Brigade after their brief secondment to 129 Brigade for the initial assault. They were ordered to move eastwards from the river, up the Gisors road, whilst the 7th Somersets kept abreast of them inside the Forest of Vernon on their left.

Over on the right-hand side of the bridgehead, Brigadier Mole likewise ordered his 129 Brigade to advance out of the small area they held around Vernonnet. The 4th Somerset Light Infantry were told to clear the forest behind and to the right of the village; then to take the next village of Bois Jérôme. To their right, the 5th Wiltshires would push inland along the road towards Gasny, whilst their sister regiment, the 4th, continued its sweep up the river valley towards Giverny.

With each hour bringing more reinforcements over the wide river and with the good news about the opening of the tank ferry, Thomas faced this, the third day of the battle, with equanimity, knowing that he was as ready as he would ever be to meet an enemy counter-attack. Throughout the division spirits were high. The morning was bright and sunny; there was no sign of the enemy and everyone, apart from the Cornwalls on the left of the lodgement, felt that the opposition had flown. The battle for the Seine was won. Unfortunately, as events later that day were to prove, there would have to be much more bloodshed before the German army was to release its hold on the Seine.

Just after 0800 hours, on the river bank above Pressagny l'Orgueilleux, two Sherman tanks, one pulling the other, ground slowly up the rise leading to the road that runs down the valley. Sergeant Reg Cox had extricated his stranded troop leader's tank from the muddy shoreline, allowing the first armour across the Seine to set off northwards in search of the infantry. Lieutenant Michael Trasenster, in the leading Sherman, still felt a little vulnerable, especially when he thought of the wide river separating him from the rest of the regiment. Later he felt even worse when he found out that the next tanks across were moving in the opposite direction, up the river valley, to reinforce the centre of the bridgehead. His two Shermans alone were to be the means of halting further enemy attacks from the north.

When Trasenster arrived at le Château de la Madeleine, he was pleased to find 214 Brigade's commander outside the house talking to Colonel Taylor. He had a high regard for Essame: '… a splendid soldier, bright and courageous in two wars, and quite tough at the sharp end of the fighting'.

The brigadier explained what he wanted from the tanks and then left it up to the tank leader. Trasenster was pleased to have been given a relatively free hand, for experience had taught him that:

There was nothing worse than being 'messed around' by some indifferent infantry commander, trying to dictate tank tactics – as sometimes happened with quite fatal results for all concerned. It was harder for NCO tank commanders to resist these dictates, for they were often dealing with quite senior officers, sometimes, as in this case, as high as brigadiers. On this occasion, however, all was well; Essame and Taylor were true professionals.

The two Shermans pulled off the road and took up positions covering the exit from the village.

The three companies of the 5th Cornwalls were still halted short of Pressagny. With the arrival of the armoured cars and the two tanks, Taylor felt secure enough to send a strong patrol into the village. This patrol was led by the armoured cars, which passed through the village and carried on out the other side into open country towards Notre Dame de l'Isle. There was no sign of the enemy; everything was quiet. Taylor then sent a company through the village with orders to set up an observation post on the far side. With them went the two Shermans from the 4th/7th Royal Dragoon Guards, together with some heavy machine-guns from the 8th Middlesex (the division's machine-gun battalion), who had just arrived to support the Cornwalls.

Since the sharp clash during the early morning darkness, there had been no German activity around Pressagny. The situation appeared outwardly to be calm, safe enough for the tank crews to join the infantry in a chat and a brew of tea. Before long, enemy troops were seen moving near the water's edge, congregating alongside a barge about 4,000 yards (3,648m) downstream. Trasenster felt that it was essential to give the impression that there were rather more tanks around than just his two, for everyone's benefit, including his own.

The two Shermans opened fire on the gathering enemy infantry, ranging their shot on the outline of the nearby black barge. They were firing shells fused at half-a-second delayed action. (This would mean that the shells would either ricochet and air burst, or penetrate a structure and then explode.) By this time in the campaign, the tank crews were superbly efficient, as Michael Trasenster recalls:

At extreme range a good loader could sometimes get four or five shells in the air at the same time, before the first one landed. The gunner kept his foot on the firing pedal and the loader kept the rounds on his lap. As the round went in, the loader kept his arm moving up and over the breech block, which closed and fired. There were risks: you lost an arm if you hesitated as the gun recoiled.

The results of the shoot were spectacular. Shells began to fall among the startled Germans. The first one air burst, the next penetrated the barge. The vessel must have been loaded with ammunition or petrol, for there was a tremendous explosion. Trasenster was watching through his field glasses and, for a fraction of a second, saw the ribs of the barge lit up in silhouette before the craft disintegrated into a ball of bright yellow flame. Both tanks then opened up with their coaxial and hull-mounted machine-guns, firing continously until they had expended almost all of their ammunition. During the long barrage, Cox's machine-gun suffered a blockage and his loader was injured whilst attempting to clear the obstruction without having time to let the gun cool down. The other tank continued to shoot until the hull machine-gun's rifling was so worn that the spiralling fire was ineffective, by which time the Germans had moved away from sight. This possible attack against the Cornwalls was therefore averted, for the enemy chose to move off inland through the thick woods, accepting the cover afforded by the Forest of Vernon. The Cornishmen had escaped a strong counter-attack against their flank – but inside that dark forest the 7th Somerset Light Infantry were not to be so fortunate.

The 7th Somersets were commanded by Lieutenant-Colonel J.W. Nichol. He had joined the battalion on Hill 112 on 13 July, becoming its third commander within three days, the other two having both been killed. Nichol went on to lead his battalion through some of the most bitter fighting of the campaign. He was a brave and popular leader, winning the DSO on the attack on le Plessis Grimault. A small, dapper man, he possessed a very clear mind, always knowing exactly what he wanted to do. Everything he said was crisp and to the point. The officers in the battalion all liked him and had great confidence in his leadership.

On the morning of 27 August, the 7th Somersets were entrenched in a tight diamond formation just inside the Forest of Vernon, to the right of the 5th DCLI. At 0800 hours the battalion received orders from the brigade commander to advance through the dense forest to the eastern edge just south of the village of Panilleuse, its objective being to make sure the whole area was clear of Germans.

Although the battalion had four companies in operation, they were all below full strength. Each of the companies contained only two platoons instead of the normal three, with the three sections in the platoon having around six instead of ten men. The situation that morning found 'B', 'C' and 'D' Companies holding the forward area of the battalion's positions, with 'A' Company at the rear.

The major commanding 'A' Company was a newcomer to the unit. Although a full major, he was still untried in action, unlike those battle-hardened veterans around him (most of the other company commanders throughout the division had found promotion extremely rapid, because of the casualties suffered during the previous two months). The new major had spent most of the war in the Colonies and, as such, lacked battle experience; in addition, the company contained many other new replacements. In view of this, Nichol intended to give 'A' Company a gradual reintroduction to the fighting.

Major-General Thomas was a commander who loved to be in close contact with the action. He always wanted to know exactly what was going on. It was his nature to spend a great deal of time swanning around visiting his brigadiers, often interfering with their decisions as a result. This once prompted Brigadier Essame to comment: 'A good gardener leaves his plants to grow on their own, and doesn't come round every couple of days to pull them up to see how the roots are growing!' Nevertheless, Thomas continued to intervene in the handling not only of battalions but even of companies, whenever he did not have enough else to do. That morning, as Major Bill Chalmers, the brigade major with 214 Brigade, recalls, Thomas visited brigade HQ to discuss the plans for the move inland with Essame. The brigade advance was outlined but Thomas was not satisfied. He picked on the fact that 'A' Company of the 7th Somersets was held back in reserve and not being used. Thomas insisted that all the companies should push through the forest and clear the woods as quickly as possible, then make for the village of Panilleuse. He told his brigadier to tell Nichol to move 'A' Company to a set of cross tracks in the middle of the Forest of Vernon.

Nichol had planned to use his three leading companies to advance on a broad front, sweeping the forest as they went, with 'A' Company as his reserve. The new orders posed a problem; it would mean a change of tactics. The broad sweep, which admittedly would take much longer, now became a narrow thrust, not necessarily clearing the forest, but merely passing through. Thomas was evidently not contemplating a counter-attack, but was anxious to enlarge the bridgehead with all speed, so as to be ready for the rest of XXX Corps to pass through. Nichol complied with the general's order and sent 'A' Company to the cross tracks, expecting the advance to be no more than a fighting patrol. The other three companies could then move forward and pass through what should by then be a firm base for the rest of the battalion.

The objective was a set of cross tracks some way in front of the forward company. On the small-scale maps available to the battalion, this junction appeared to be the crossing point for the two main rides through the forest: the route north that the Somersets were advancing up, and an east–west track that stretched from le Château de la Madeleine near Pressagny (the 5th DCLI HQ) to the village of Bois Jérôme, away to the south-east. Just off the objective were some farm buildings. The distance from the 7th Somersets' start line was about twelve hundred yards. To add to the problems of map-reading, the woods were criss-crossed with numerous smaller rides and firebreaks, most of which were not marked on the available map. At around 1000 hours, 'A' Company set off down the long straight that led to its objective.

The road to Gisors runs north-east out of Vernonnet, following the line of the deep valley between the right-hand and middle spurs overlooking the Seine. The road clings to the eastern side of this steep re-entrant, taking a winding course through the thickly wooded countryside. On the right of the road the ground rises sharply, whilst that to the left falls away to the valley bottom. Visibility on either side, once off the road, was only twenty yards. The next village, about three miles (4.8km) away, was called Tilly.

At an 'orders' group early that morning, the commander of the 1st Worcestershires, Lieutenant-Colonel Robert Osborne-Smith, had been instructed by Brigadier Essame to advance his battalion up the Gisors road and capture Tilly. There was not expected to be any significant resistance. In the event, the Worcestershires were never to get within two miles (3km) of the village.

Like all the other battalions in the division, the 1st Worcestershires were sadly depleted after the savage fighting of the earlier Normandy battles. Their strength was down from over a thousand to only 553 men. This included a large percentage of reinforcements from other units. Each rifle company averaged 65 men and consisted of just two platoons and an enlarged company headquarters.

In view of the thick undergrowth and the steep sloping sides of the valley, the only way the battalion could move was up the main road. Consequently, orders were given for the regiment to proceed in the normal advance-to-contact formation. 'D' Company was to lead, supported by a troop of armoured cars from the reconnaissance regiment and a troop of tanks from the 4th/7th Royal Dragoon Guards. With these leading infantry were some of the battalion's own supporting arms, pioneers and a section of the carrier platoon. The battalion's mortars were to be off-loaded and 'in action' at the start line, located in a clearing to the right of the road, with the anti-tank guns alongside ready to move forward. The remainder of the battalion was to follow, with Major Algy Grubb's 'B' Company in the rear.

It was the practice in the battalion that if a company had been in contact with the enemy, then they went to the back of the queue in the next action. The trouble in which Grubb had been involved the previous afternoon (which would not have happened had he been on the right track) now resulted in his company being placed in reserve for the advance. His impression that morning was that they were all on a nice little summer's walk up a country road.

At 0810 hours, just as the Worcestershires were moving off, news came through that there would not be any tanks supporting the advance. The first two Shermans over the river had gone to help the 5th Cornwalls in Pressagny; others would hopefully join the battalion later that morning. Undaunted, the regiment set off up the main road without its supporting armour.

Just ten minutes later the commander of the leading platoon fell wounded, hit by an enemy machine-gun sited just off the road. Seconds later another man fell. The advance halted. 'D' Company went to ground on both sides of the road whilst the machine-gun was located. Then the 3in mortars were called on to plaster the area with bombs and an attack was put in by the leading platoon. The enemy post fell silent. At 0920 hours the advance continued.

General Thomas had ordered that all six battalions which were over the river should advance inland that morning. 129 Brigade now started its move. The ground to the right of the 1st Worcestershires was the province of the 4th

Somerset Light Infantry. Its objective that day was the village of Bois Jérôme St Ouen. Its course was to take it through the southern part of the Forest of Vernon. Once again, the maps available to the unit were of small scale, making it difficult to select a clear route. However, the Maquis were able to supply two guides, one of whom, a Monsieur Giret, spoke perfect English with a slight cockney accent. He seemed to know all about the German dispositions in the area and the best route to take, as the battalion history explains:

> The Colonel was suspicious. We had been warned of plausible enemy spies. 'You had better come with us,' said the Colonel. 'Righto, I'll just tell the old woman I'll be out for lunch' was the reply. He travelled in the Commanding Officer's carrier. His prophecies were subsequently proved to be correct and his behaviour under fire, with the prospect at one time of capture by the Hun while in civilian clothes, was admirable and a credit to the organisation he worked for.

The 4th Somersets began their advance with 'B' Company, led by the Maquis guide, at their head. The route was along a dusty road overgrown with vegetation, which soon became narrow and winding with many small tracks leading off on either side. Before long, the following company, 'D' Company, had managed to become separated from the rest of the battalion in the thick undergrowth and had run into trouble, coming under a considerable amount of enemy fire. The company had stumbled upon two dug-in tanks backed up by German infantry. The tanks proved to be old obsolete examples, used in a static defensive role to add firepower to a strong-point blocking the way to the village. The opposition was so fierce that 'D' Company was forced to a halt and went to ground for protection. It reported its plight to battalion HQ and was told to disengage and rejoin the main axis. The strong-point could wait until after the capture of Bois Jérôme, when it could be mopped up from the rear. In the meantime, 'B' Company had arrived at a château in the woods just short of the village; it was occupied by the enemy.

Further over to the right of the 4th Somersets, the two Wiltshire battalions were beginning their advance that morning: the 5th was sweeping along the Gasny road out of Vernonnet, whilst the 4th was moving southwards along the cliffs overlooking the river. Before long, they both came up against German opposition. The 5th Wiltshires met the strongest resistance, being halted after only a very short distance by a self-propelled 37mm anti-aircraft gun, mounted on an 8-ton half-track, being used in a ground support role.

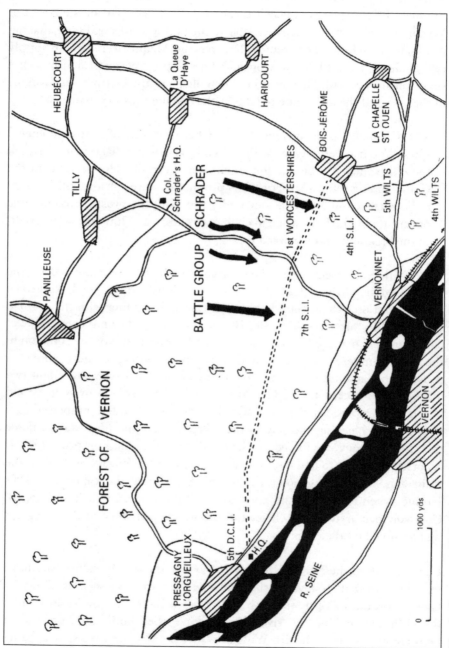

Map 8. Counter-attack by Battle Group Schrader.

The six Wessex battalions had all once again made contact with the enemy, who were still there close by the Seine. The German commander of the 49th Infantry Division, General Macholtz, had taken firmer control of the situation. His orders for an immediate counter-attack the previous night had arrived too late for a concerted effort, but he had, nevertheless, managed to reorganise what troops he had available to him to present a united front against further expansion. By morning, the resistance on all sides of the lodgement area had stiffened. Macholtz was now ready to launch his counter-attack proper, just at a time when most of the British opposition felt that the Germans had shot their bolt and were retreating pell-mell for the Fatherland.

To launch his attack, General Macholtz had assembled various units from the 149th and 150th Grenadier Regiments, together with some from the division's 149th Fusilier Battalion, and had placed them under the command of Colonel Schrader. Schrader had his headquarters in the Château Saulseuses, situated just two miles (3km) along the Gisors road up which the 1st Worcestershires were advancing. At 1020 that morning, he issued an operational order for the attack. Specific objectives were laid down for the battle group. Coincidentally, at that same moment, three of the advancing British battalions were heading for those same objectives: on the German left, 1/Division Fusilier Battalion 149 was ordered to secure the edge of the wood west of Bois Jérôme; the 4th Somersets were also heading for this same area prior to their attack on the village. In the centre of the German attack came the main thrust down the Gisors to Vernonnet road, supported by three Tiger tanks from the 205th Heavy Tank Battalion; this would inevitably meet the 1st Worcestershires head on coming up the road. On the right of the German attack, Schrader had ordered that the track running from le Château de la Madeleine through the Forest of Vernon should be secured as the first prime objective. Sadly, this was the very spot that the inexperienced 'A' Company of the 7th Somersets had hoped to settle on. The results were to be devastating.

Situation at 1000 Hours Sunday 27 August
Thomas's two brigades were at last beginning to expand the bridgehead. With the tank ferry now in use, there was armour over the river to help cope with any German counter-attack, although there were no indications that the enemy was about to launch one. Back in Vernon, the 43rd Division's third brigade, 130 Brigade, was assembling ready to be passed over the river and into the bridgehead when it was needed. Bridging operations were continuing on the first Bailey so as to be ready for the remainder of the troops of XXX Corps, who were at that moment closing on the town. Things were looking good for Thomas.

Chapter 15

Counter-Attack

'A' Company of the 7th Somerset Light Infantry was lost, although this fact, at that moment, was unknown to its men. The company had reached a large set of cross tracks which the commander believed was the objective and had radioed the news back to HQ. Up until that point, the Somersets had met no opposition. The two platoons quickly set about digging in, so as to prepare a firm base from which the rest of the battalion would advance to the edge of the forest. They were widely dispersed in the dense woods, sited to cover the area of the cross tracks and the nearby farm – but it was the wrong farm at the wrong junction.

The company had in fact passed over the set of cross tracks on the main ride that led to le Château de la Madeleine and had advanced several hundred yards further on, finding more tracks and another farm which the men believed to be their objective. It was an understandable mistake, for in the dense woods one track looked much like any other. It was very difficult to decide just what constituted a main ride from all the other little tracks and paths that criss-crossed the thick vegetation. This was understandable certainly, but also unfortunate, for the area near the farm soon came under mortar fire from the advancing Battle Group Schrader.

'A' Company quickly made contact once again with battalion HQ to explain its sudden plight. The mortaring continued and was joined by machine-gun fire as the enemy moved closer. These new weapons helped the company commander to pinpoint the source of this fire away to his left, allowing a location to be radioed back to the artillery. The 25-pounder field guns across the river responded at once. Shells began to fall through the trees as an artillery barrage was put down on the enemy machine-gun's reported positions. The shells did no damage to the Battle Group Schrader; it was not there. 'A' Company reported back that, as far as they could tell, the barrage had fallen near the enemy troops, but not on them.

Following behind 'A' Company was 'C' Company, commanded by Major David Durie. It had advanced towards the positions held by the leading company, but was still well short of the original set of cross tracks. Nichol suggested that Durie send a fighting patrol forward to find out just what was happening to his leading troops. Meanwhile, the next company due to set off from battalion HQ, 'D' Company, was told to hold fast until more information was received.

The fighting patrol from 'C' Company soon reached the main cross tracks and found the area deserted. The information was hurriedly relayed back to Major Durie and then on to Nichol; 'A' Company was not there. Hardly had this message been received when 'A' Company came back on the air to report that it was surrounded and urgently needed reinforcements. Nichol reacted quickly; a troop of tanks from the 4th/7th Royal Dragoon Guards had just arrived with the Somersets and the commander sent the Shermans straight on through the forest to the aid of his beleaguered infantry, with 'D' Company hard on their heels. A second message from 'A' Company said that things were serious, but it thought that it could deal with the attack. Nichol replied that tanks were on their way. The signal was never acknowledged.

The situation at battalion HQ became very tense as the staff there waited for news from the forward company. Then quite soon, to everyone's relief, the tanks radioed back that they had reached the troops and were engaging the enemy. It looked as though the moment had been saved. However, ten minutes later another message came through, this time from Durie's 'C' Company, stating that the company had been joined by a troop of tanks which were fighting with it against a large party of the enemy who had suddenly appeared. The Dragoon Guards had obviously only made it to the first set of cross tracks. 'A' Company was still on its own.

When he realised his mistake, Colonel Nichol urged the tanks to push on towards the isolated company. They tried but they did not get far: the leading tank lost its commander, who was killed, and the other two Shermans got into difficulties in the dense undergrowth. The relief ground to a halt.

By this time, 'D' Company was up at the first cross tracks and sent a patrol on to help the tanks. It, too, was soon involved in fierce fighting, quickly taking a considerable number of casualties. Battle Group Schrader continued to press forward, forcing the tanks and the infantry to withdraw to the cross tracks. The Somersets were now in serious trouble; far from advancing, they were hard pressed to hold their ground. There was no longer any hope of reaching the isolated 'A' Company; it was evident that it had been completely over–run.

At the cross tracks, the two surviving companies desperately tried to hold on to the situation. It was early afternoon before the position began to steady. The Somersets found themselves deeply embroiled in a particularly difficult type of fighting, as Major David Durie recalls:

In the thick woods, you could never see the enemy. When, suddenly, the fire came at you from out of the trees, everyone immediately went to ground and started to blaze away with Bren guns in all directions. Then we began edging forward firing like mad, trying to identify where the enemy fire was coming from. It was a slow process, made even more difficult by the presence of enemy snipers. Nevertheless, we had one great asset with us in the shape of the forward artillery observer. Once we had identified an enemy location, we would contact him to get details passed back to the guns. It was very frightening to be in a forest when the shells arrived, the danger being not only from the shrapnel, but also from branches and whole trees crashing down. It was certainly discouraging for the enemy.

The 7th Somerset Light Infantry had been fought to a standstill. They could get no further forward than the first set of cross tracks. A complete company had been lost, whilst two other companies had taken serious casualties, but the line had held. The right flank of Battle Group Schrader's attack had also been halted here in the forest. The Germans were to make no more progress along this route. It was late in the afternoon before the attack finally petered out, too late, and too risky, for the Somersets to try any further advance, for, less than a mile away to their right, they could hear the sounds of another stiff action taking place. The 1st Worcestershires had also run into Battle Group Schrader on the Gisors road.

'D' Company, leading the Worcestershires' advance up the twisting road out of Vernonnet through the densely wooded terrain, had halted. The leading platoon could hear tank tracks. They sent a patrol forward and it was confirmed that a Tiger tank could be seen on the road a few hundred yards ahead, together with a party of Germans.

All foot soldiers fear tanks and, in the Allied army, everyone feared Tiger tanks most of all. In consequence, every enemy tank became a Tiger. They had achieved a position of awe in the minds of the troops. The Tiger was virtually invincible. Its thick armour and large 88mm gun made it capable of withstanding the fire of any Allied tank and all anti-tank guns (bar the 17-pounder) except at suicidally short ranges. All large German tanks – Panthers, Mark IVs and even some self-propelled guns – were often mistakenly labelled as being Tigers by the British infantry. However, this time it was true; there was a Tiger coming down the road and it was heading straight for the Worcestershires.

The carrier section dismounted and moved off the road up the steep ground on the right to protect that flank, whilst the second platoon moved

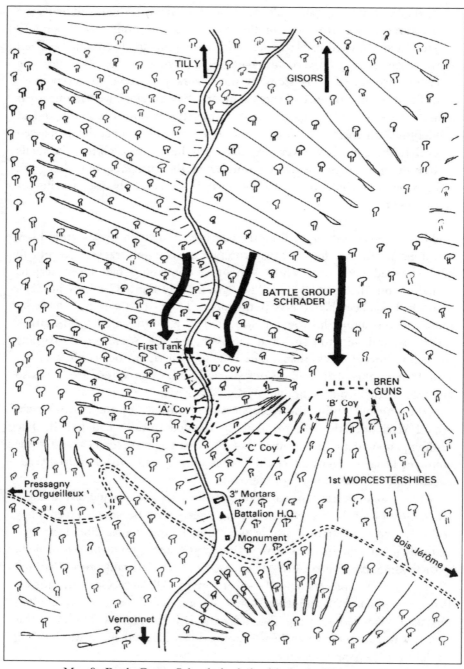

Map 9. Battle Group Schrader's clash with the 1st Worcestershires.

forward with its PIAT to engage the Tiger. The platoon tried to find a suitable position along the verges, but the road itself was the only flat area around. On either side the ground was steep, rising to the right and falling away to the left; there was no room to deploy the PIAT. It would be disastrous to engage the Tiger as it came round the corner into sight. From such an exposed position on the road, the poor man firing the weapon would have to be at almost point-blank range. The chances of his survival were nil. The second platoon reported back that it was unable to engage the tank.

It was now up to the two 6-pounder anti-tank guns with the leading company to deal with the tank. They went into action on the road, one covering the bend whilst the other held a position a hundred yards further back.

The 6-pounder anti-tank guns were part of the battalion's own armament. The purpose of these light, manoeuvrable guns was to give firepower up with the leading troops, just where it was needed. When first issued to infantry divisions in 1942, the gun performed exceptionally well, and was capable of knocking out any of the lightly armoured Axis tanks, but by August 1944 it was unable to breach the thicker defences of the latest German Tigers and Panthers.

The 6-pounder was capable of penetrating 74mm of armour at 1,000 yards (914m) when firing a solid six pound shot of steel. The front armour of a Tiger was 100mm thick. However, a recent British development in shell manufacture had produced a 'sabot' projectile, specifically designed for anti-tank use. It was composed of a small solid tungsten core in a light steel sheath. The shell was then built up to the six pound calibre by attaching a four-piece light alloy sabot jacket. The purpose of the sabot unit was to produce a shell of normal calibre but lighter weight and yet still having a very dense core, capable of penetrating thick armour. As the shell left the muzzle of the gun after firing, the sabot jacket was discarded and fell away, leaving the tungsten shot to continue to the target. The shell was thus able to achieve much higher velocities than a conventional shell, capable of penetrating 146mm of armour plate at 1,000 yards. Luckily, the Worcestershires' 6-pounders that day were loaded with sabot shell.

With his sights set firmly on the bend around which the tank must come, the anti-tank gun's aimer waited. The gun was loaded, the range adjusted, virtually at point-blank, and it was ready. On either side of the road, the infantry had deployed and was poised. The signal for the start of the show would be the appearance of the villain of the piece, the Tiger.

Slowly, noisily, the 56-ton monster ground round the corner. With no more than the off-side of the hull and the turret visible, the gunner opened fire. The first shell hit and penetrated the mantlet surrounding the tank's 88mm gun. In a few seconds the 6-pounder was reloaded and fired again: another hit, then again, another hit, both times in the hull. The Tiger was beaten. The surviving crew quickly started to bale out of the stricken, useless hulk. The 6-pounder continued to fire, this time using high-explosive shells. There was an explosion and the tank burst into flames. The crew were all killed; one lay draped half in, half out of the turret. The sudden demise of the tank was too much for its supporting escort of infantry; they hurriedly withdrew.

The introduction of enemy tanks into the action added a new dimension to the battle of the bridgehead. Brigade HQ told Colonel Osborne-Smith to halt his battalion where it was. It was increasingly evident that the enemy was engaging in a counter-attack of some strength. Other battalions on both sides of the Worcestershires were being delayed in their advance by the same German battle group. The move up the Gisors road was halted until tanks could be brought up from the ferry site. The Colonel then moved 'C' Company forward on to the high ground on the right, to stop any enemy attempt to infiltrate that flank. 'D' Company was told to consolidate where it was astride the road, whilst 'A' Company held a similar position behind them. 'B' Company, under Major Algy Grubb, was in reserve further back down the road in a 'layby' with the mortars.

About a mile from Vernonnet, along the Gisors road, is a small clearing on the right-hand side. Standing fifty feet from the road is a pointed obelisk, its shape not unlike Cleopatra's Needle on the banks of the Thames. Erected in the eighteenth century, it commemorates a local dignitary. That Sunday morning, 'B' Company was halted around this clearing, which also happened to be the site of battalion HQ. Algy Grubb had his shirt off and was beside his company carrier in the process of having a shave in the sunshine.

I could hear some commotion going on further up the road but felt that it was nothing for me to worry about, after all my company was number four in the queue. The first thing that attracted my attention was men coming back down the road. There was great panic, then a bullet ricocheted off the top of this monument alongside which I was standing, knocking down a great lump of stone. The bullet carried on and went through the head of a carrier driver, killing him instantly. I thought to myself 'To hell with this!' Then things really started to boil up!

Battle Group Schrader had managed to infiltrate both flanks and was engaging 'D' Company with machine-guns. The fire was coming at the

Worcestershires from out of the thick undergrowth, making it difficult to pinpoint; it was both heavy and accurate. The carrier section was pinned down on the right, losing its commander, who was killed. All around, the enemy continued to press forward, the intensity of its machine-gun fire increasing. The Germans soon overtook the leading platoon of the Worcestershires and began enfilading their positions from both sides. Casualties quickly began to mount. The second platoon was likewise engaged by more unlocated enemy to the left of the road. It countered this fire with the help of an armoured car whose heavy machine-gun fired continually into the trees, sweeping the area, searching for the unseen enemy. Then a message from the leading platoon reported that a second Tiger tank was moving down the road. 'D' Company was in real danger of being over-run.

Although the enemy soldiers on either side could not be seen, their approximate locations were known. Word was passed back to the mortars and artillery and soon trees and undergrowth on both sides of the road began erupting into flames, as high-explosive shells crashed down. Any likely gathering places were given as targets, with the hope of keeping the enemy on the move. The whole of the left flank was on a lower level, overlooked by everyone on the road right back to battalion HQ. It was a simple matter for all available guns to keep pouring an incredible amount of fire down into the valley. To Colonel Osborne-Smith, this side was not seen as the main danger; he could confidently stop any enemy movement along the densely wooded valley. His most immediate problem was the high ground on the right and the commanding hilltop in particular. He already had 'C' Company up there on the slopes, but this hill still seemed to be wide open to any enemy flanking movement.

Major Grubb had also spotted the danger. He had no doubt that the narrow road was not the place to be; he felt that down there you could not stop anything and in any case there were far too many bodies already milling around. Grubb decided to take his company up onto the hill.

Algy Grubb was a company commander who believed in a certain amount of theatre to keep his men going. He tried to give a 'larger than life' impression in the way he approached things. Experience had taught him that the private soldier would always stand firm if his officers were there with him when things became serious, especially if the officer was outwardly showing little concern at events. Grubb had two personal bodyguards: Joe Cook, his sixth batman since arriving in France (who, incidentally, made it through the rest of the war with him) and George Bromwich, a dustman from Leamington Spa. Bromwich was unique; he had never done a day's training in his life. He was the company bootmaker and turned out to be one of the finest soldiers Grubb had ever come across. The major never went anywhere without the two of them. 'When you saw us going along with a trailer, with all the guns you could think of – not that we could use many of them – it looked just like Al Capone.'

Grubb's task was to stop any of the enemy who tried to come through the woods on the hilltop, and he had already decided just how he would do it:

> I intended to collect all my company's Bren guns together and string them up so that anyone who came over the hill could bloody well have it. We had thirteen Bren guns and four 2in mortars in the company. An exercise we had performed at the Infantry Training School was to demonstrate the firepower of a battalion. We would line up the whole battalion along a ridge in front of some water and then get everyone to fire their weapons at the same time. It was an impressive sight to see the water erupt into millions of fountains. Somehow I could see all that in my mind and so I decided that if I grouped all my firepower together, then the enemy would have a bit of a job to get through.

In effect, Grubb split his company into two groups, as opposed to the normal structure of three platoons. He decided to lead the first group to the top of the hill, whilst his second-in-command, Captain Noel Watkins, came up behind with the riflemen and took up a position just short of the crest.

> I took the company HQ's Bren gun myself, whilst my two 'bodyguards' carried my ammunition. The hill was very steep, thick with trees at the bottom near the road, then a grassy slope and finally another sprinkling of trees at the top. At the bottom of the hill, the battalion's 3in mortars were lined up under the control of Jock Bannister. They were in the layby near the monument. The mortars were pumping the stuff over the top of the hill. They had been firing continuously and they had all overheated. What was happening was that as soon as a mortar bomb was put into the barrel, its primary charge was igniting and the bombs were falling only twenty yards away. This in itself was safe enough, for there has to be a projection of 'X' yards before the bomb is fused and could explode, but the mortars somehow had to be cooled down. Jock Bannister lined up his men and got them to pee on the barrels by numbers! As we set off up the slope, I shouted to Jock to keep the bloody things going!

Halfway up the hill Grubb was surprised to see a company dug in. This was the third company, 'C' Company. The company commander was as surprised to see Grubb as Grubb was to see him. They didn't say anything, but it did occur to Grubb that it was rather a silly place to be and he thought that it was something and nothing in such a position. At, or about, that moment and close by the mortars, Grubb met Major Tony Benn, the battalion's second-in-command. He was a regular soldier of the East Yorkshire Regiment, who had joined the battalion a fortnight earlier. Grubb had got to know him well and greatly admired him. Benn remarked that the whole action had developed into chaos, as was usual, and asked Grubb what he was going to do about it. Grubb replied that he was taking his company up on top of the hill. 'I reckon that that's about right, mate,' Benn replied and set off down towards the road. It was the last time Grubb was to see his friend.

Down on the main road, the leading company was being pressed by a second Tiger, moving slowly forward into their positions. The tank's machine-gun was firing at the British infantry dispersed along the verges and amongst the trees. This time it was the Tiger that had the upper hand. The anti-tank gun covering the road, the same one that had been so successful just a short while earlier, was being harassed by yet another enemy machine-gun. Accurate fire was forcing the gun crew to keep their heads down. Manoeuvring cautiously round the previously knocked-out German tank, the second Tiger turned on the exposed 6-pounder before the small gun could get off a shot. The shell from the tank's massive 88mm barrel smashed into the Worcestershires' gun, reducing it to a pile of twisted metal, killing all the crew. Next, the German heavy locked its sights on the 6-pounder's carrier; that too disintegrated into a pall of smoke and flame. A few moments later another blinding flash and a heavy armoured car from the reconnaissance regiment met the same fate.

To match an armoured car against the heaviest of German tanks was no match at all. Just this one shell from the Tiger blasted the car off the road. Amazingly, Sergeant Barraclough and the crew all scrambled out safely with no more damage to their persons than superficial injuries and a severe shaking. The great tank continued to lumber on down the road unchecked, seemingly invincible.

The German tank was carving its way into the heart of 'D' Company. The leading platoon had already suffered thirty per cent casualties, including their commander. There was no room for the British infantry to deploy off the road, for the company had been forced to halt at an awkward spot not of their own choosing. With the arrival of this second tank, their position had become untenable. Permission was requested for a withdrawal; it was immediately granted. The company was ordered to pull back through 'A' Company to a new position where it could establish a much firmer base.

Back at battalion HQ there was better news. A troop of Sherman tanks from the 4th/7th Royal Dragoon Guards had arrived from the ferry site. One of the tanks was a Sherman Firefly, sporting the mighty 17-pounder gun. Given the right opportunity and a bit of luck, it could be a match for the Tiger. In one of the other tanks was 'A' Squadron's commander, Major Jackie Goldsmid. After getting the latest news from the battalion commander, Goldsmid sent the Firefly up the road with a view to engaging the German tank, should it get too close to the battalion HQ.

Meanwhile, the Tiger had halted on the road to wait for its protecting infantry to keep abreast of it (they were trying to push through on the Worcestershires' right flank, on the slopes of the hill). Every vehicle in sight on that short stretch of highway was destroyed. The stationary Tiger had become the complete master of the battlefield.

Even though the tank had halted, the hull machine-gun kept up a non-stop stream of bullets sweeping along the road and its verges. With great difficulty, word was passed forward for 'D' Company to begin its withdrawal to a more secure part of the road. At this point, the battalion was most vulnerable.

In ones and twos, hugging closely to any cover that was available, the infantry from 'D' Company tried to slip back down the road. During training, a withdrawal is conducted under very strict drill; the whole exercise is accomplished bit by bit, everyone covering each other. In reality, a battle progresses in perfect chaos. Seldom, in action, does anything ever go right; so it was on this occasion. 'D' Company had to pass through 'A' Company', which was dug in to the rear on either side of the road. The men started to fall back through the trees that lined the steep verges. Once clear of the enemy, they moved a little more openly, a little faster. Behind them was the rattle of the Tiger's machine-gun and the roar of its engine. The men of 'A' Company were suddenly confronted by their own troops hurriedly withdrawing through their lines and heading for the rear. It was too much for some of them; they jumped up and joined in what, on the face of it, appeared to be a general retreat.

For a few moments, control was lost. Some of the infantry were running back down the road, others were moving quite openly through the trees on the right-hand side. Major Tony Benn, the battalion's second-in-command, tried to regain order. He stood up in the open, urging the men off the exposed road and back into cover. At that same moment, the Tiger started to move forward and rounded the bend, turning its machine-gun fire on those men in the road. Caught in the open, they were mown down like skittles. Regardless of the danger around him, Major Benn cursed and bullied the fleeing troops to a halt, forcing them to stand firm and cover the road. It was one of those selfless acts of heroism that was sometimes needed to steady an awkward situation. The officer set a brave example. Brave but tragic, for, just as order had been restored, Benn was hit. He died instantly.

Watching the whole episode from near his tank was Major Goldsmid, who remembers Benn as 'a very brave and courageous man'. He saw the effect that Benn had on the panic-stricken Worcestershires and was deeply impressed by the way he restored order. He was also saddened by the sudden death of the officer just as he had taken control of the rout.

The Tiger once again came to a halt in the middle of the road and waited. The Worcestershires immediately opened up with small arms fire, peppering the tank's thick armour with bullets. They could do no harm to the four inches of hardened steel that protected the German crew, but their attention served to illustrate how vulnerable the tank now was, being so far ahead of its protecting infantry. The Tiger quickly reversed back round the corner and stopped. Everything on the main road now seemed to pause whilst both sides took stock of the situation.

The two advancing columns had met each other head on and it did not seem likely that either side was going any further along the road that day. However, up on the hilltop on the Worcestershires' right flank, Battle Group Schrader was still pressing forward.

Near the top of the hill, just below the crest, Major Grubb laid out his Bren guns behind a small bank. He positioned himself in the centre and his four 2in mortars six paces behind. There was no sign of life, no firing, nothing. There was clearly nobody there. He hadn't been there long before Captain Noel Watkins sidled up and lay down beside him. Grubb asked where the riflemen were and Watkins replied that they were still at the bottom of the hill. Grubb's orders had been misunderstood; Watkins had come up alone to find out what was happening and join in the fun.

Grubb then put his head up and looked around and sank down; there was still nothing to be seen. He then broke one of his own golden rules; he looked up over the bank in exactly the same place again.

One of the basic lessons of infantry fieldcraft, one that was religiously taught everywhere, was this: get down, crawl away from where you were, observe the enemy, then fire. Down, crawl, observe, fire. This was because if you were under enemy observation, went down, then lifted your head in the same place again, the enemy could be waiting for you. As Major Grubb had stressed over and over to thousands of trainees at infantry training school, where he was once an instructor, NEVER look up in the same place twice. However, on top of the hill that day he forgot his own maxim; he did look up twice in the same place and the consequences were exactly as he had warned others. A burst of machine-gun fire raked the top of the bank. For the first time since landing in France, Grubb was hit, but Algy Grubb was a man who was born lucky and his gift did not desert him that day.

I could never get on with a steel helmet, I don't think anyone really could, because they cut into your head so. Now, the regimental hatter of the Worcestershire Regiment was Thomas & Stone in Jermyn Street. They made nice hats. They also made what looked like a polo helmet, although not as big, which was in fact a skull cap made of cork. You were measured for it and it fitted exactly. It had pieces of rubber tubing sewn on around the base to cushion the steel helmet which rested on top. With this cork skull cap you could wear the steel helmet all day long, just like a cloth cap.

The first bullet hit Grubb right in the middle of the front of the helmet and went straight through. It then hit the cork skull cap and was deflected upwards, furrowing along the cork until it finally went out through the top of the helmet. The second bullet passed through his coat collar and set fire to his tunic. The force of the bullet's impact bowled him over and knocked him out. The enemy machine-gun was only fifteen paces away, shielded behind a mound.

Major Grubb came to a few seconds later to find himself staring at a German stick grenade just a short distance away from him. Then some more came over, all landing quite close by. It was too late to do anything but press himself flat into the dirt. 'If you laid flat as possible you were usually safe, the blast normally went upwards. We used to demonstrate this during training. We would put balloons down and let off grenades near them. Rarely would a balloon burst. As long as you kept your head and laid flat, you were usually OK.'

One grenade exploded, then another and another. Grubb by this time felt that the whole thing was somehow becoming a personal little battle, with him on the receiving end. He called for all the grenades and started throwing them, but he couldn't get the range. (It was difficult to throw a grenade lying down, unlike the German stick grenades, which had a long handle; they could be thrown a good distance from a prone position.)

On the spur of the moment he ordered Captain Watkins to take command of the Bren guns and then crawled back to his 2in mortars. He took over one himself, directing the crews of the others to pass him the ammunition. The range was only about twenty yards and this necessitated the barrel of the weapon being almost perpendicular (a very hazardous thing to do with a mortar). The first 'ranging' shot he fired fell almost on top of him, landing just behind the mortar! After firing numerous other bombs a little more accurately, he crawled back to the Brens. Without knowing it, he had hit the target, an MG 42 machine-gun and its crew. It later transpired that this gun was being operated by the German company commander and so a situation had developed whereby the two opposing company commanders had engaged each other in a grenade-throwing match.

It is interesting to note, as Watkins reported later to Grubb, that the Bren gunners thought that their major was deserting them when he moved back to the mortars. They were singularly restive and Watkins had some difficulty in composing them.

The visibility on top of the hill was around forty yards (36m), sometimes as low as twenty yards (18m), owing to the thick undergrowth and trees. It was perfect country for the enemy to infiltrate small parties armed with light machine-guns. They now began to gather in strength ready to push forward over the top of the hill. Fire came at 'B' Company from all parts of the summit. Still unseen, the German battle group edged its way closer.

Major Grubb's plan had gone a little awry; his riflemen were at the bottom of the hill just when he needed them most. However, he did still have the firepower of his Bren guns available, to produce the 'wall of fire' he had envisaged earlier. Watkins was told to keep up a non-stop barrage of fire into the woods on the hilltop, whilst Grubb took himself and his two bodyguards (Bromwich and Cook) on their own flanking movement round the enemy-held summit. As soon as the Brens opened up, the intrepid three-man attack crawled off into the undergrowth.

The noise rose to a crescendo. The Bren guns fired and fired and fired continually, sweeping the whole top of the hill. The Worcestershires did not need to see the enemy; they put up such a curtain of fire that not even the bravest German would dare enter. On and on they fired, not letting up for a moment. It was enough; the attack over the top of the hill was stopped. The enemy had to pull back.

Grubb's little party had less success. They soon reached a point where they were about to show themselves and move in, but could not do so because of all the firing. Some tanks down on the main road were also sweeping the hillside with their fire. To have stood up would have been suicidal. The trio remained stranded until nightfall, when a search party from another company was sent to find them on the orders of the CO.

Situation at 1500 Hours Sunday 27 August

The main weight of the attack by Battle Group Schrader had been launched against the northern and eastern sides of the bridgehead. So far it had been stopped. Away on the 43rd Division's right flank more troops were in action. The introduction of Tiger tanks into the battle caused some alarm to General Thomas, but he remained confident that the lodgement was now sufficiently large to absorb such a shock. He had enough tanks and anti-tank guns over the river for the division to give a good account of itself. In addition, there was the comforting thought of a complete brigade of infantry available in reserve should he need it. The next few hours would surely see the climax of the battle and determine its outcome, one way or another. Thomas could only wait.

Chapter 16

The Division Holds Firm

By mid-afternoon, Battle Group Schrader had reached the high point of its attack. On the left of the Forest of Vernon, the 7th Somersets had lost a company, but had stalled that part of the German advance. To the right, up on the hill, Grubb and his 'B' Company had stopped the enemy's encircling movement with their wall of Bren-gun fire. Down on the main road, the way had been blocked by British tanks and infantry. The second Tiger remained where it was, covered by enemy infantry which had moved up to join it, but not daring to move round the next bend. The trees on both sides of the road were being continually sprayed by heavy machine-gun fire from the British tanks. Both advances, the 43rd Division's up the road and the German's down in the opposite direction, had been suspended; each side halted where it was.

Earlier that day, during the middle of the morning, the battalion to the right of the Worcestershires, the 4th Somersets, was approaching Bois Jérôme. 'B' Company had arrived at a small château a little way short of the village. It was occupied by the enemy, but a surprise attack by the Somersets quickly evicted them, suffering the loss of four men in the process. Once in possession, Captain Hutchinson, who was still in command of 'B' Company, was told to hand over the château to the carrier platoon and then proceed towards the village to try to gain a lodgement. Hutchinson left one platoon to hold the house until the carrier platoon arrived, whilst he moved back into the woods to plan his next move.

'D' Company, which had met opposition during its advance through the woods, had still not yet rejoined the rest of the battalion. It was engaged in a wide encircling movement through the woods in search of the main body. At that same time, some of the enemy who had caused the hold-up were now themselves withdrawing in a straight line back to Bois Jérôme. These retreating Germans now came upon the château just as the platoon from 'B' Company was handing over to the carrier platoon. It was the Somersets' turn to be taken by surprise; they were evicted from the house and lost two more men killed. The Germans were once more in occupation.

To make matters worse for the battalion, the rear two companies, 'A' and 'C', now came under fire. Their left flank was being subjected to a heavy attack from out of the woods. They were in fact being pressed by the right flank of the Battle Group Schrader, which was launching its counter-attack against this side of the bridgehead. The German 149 Fusilier Battalion was after control of the same area of forest. Captain Hutchinson recalls:

> The first I knew of our troubles was when one of our fellows from the château rushed up and said, 'The Jerries are in behind us'. When the CO heard the news, he immediately ordered my company to retake the château at all costs. It was a sticky problem, for surrounding the house was a wire fence and a wall. The only way through was the gate. At that time we had three armoured cars up with us and so I asked one of them if he could blow a hole in the wall of the château. The moment he had done that, I planned to rush through the gate with all my company; it seemed the only way. However, I do remember thinking to myself, 'My God, what if the gate is covered by a machine-gun?' I was going to send the whole bunch of about forty men through that one gate. I told them that once they were through, to spread out quickly and get around the back. I must admit though, I was worried about the consequences of rushing that gate.

In the event, nothing untoward happened. The enemy had pulled out, continuing their retreat towards Bois Jérôme. 'B' Company was able to reoccupy the château unopposed. The 4th Somersets were now caught in something of a dilemma. On the one hand, the original German defenders in front of them were pulling out, whilst, at the same time, they were being attacked in their rear by Battle Group Schrader.

This enemy counter-attack was causing some concern to Lieutenant-Colonel Lipscombe. His battalion was in real danger of being cut off from the rest of the division. He found himself having to organise the defence of his rear companies strung out in the forest, just as he was preparing for his own attack against the village of Bois Jérôme. He therefore ordered Hutchinson to consolidate his hold on the château and the surrounding area, whilst he sent the three armoured cars back to help 'A' and 'C' Companies.

The armoured cars were of great assistance to the hard-pressed infantry. Their almost silent approach caught many of the enemy unawares. Those of the attackers who did not run away were mown down by the cars' machine-guns. The German battle group had no anti-tank guns with them, relying solely on light cannon and machine-guns, and so the cars of the reconnaissance regiment had little to worry about, just as long as they had friendly infantry around them for protection. The presence of these armoured cars effectively halted the German battle group, the combination of thick forest and heavy fire blunting their attack. Nevertheless, the enemy's 20mm cannon were extremely dangerous weapons, causing many casualties from their small shells bursting among the trees above the Somersets' heads.

All the while the enemy counter-attack was in progress against the Somersets, the 94th Field Regiment's artillery continued to harass the Germans each time a location was passed back to them from the forward observation officers. Once again, it was extremely difficult to locate the enemy in the dense woods, most of the ranging being done by sound. Back across the river, the regiment's 25-pounders were still emplaced in the Forest of Bizy, in the same positions from which they had supported the initial assault. With the move inland by the infantry of 129 Brigade (the brigade which the 94th Field Regiment normally fought with) the guns too needed to change their positions to be nearer the fighting.

Earlier that day, a survey party led by the regiment's second-in-command, Major Michael Concannon, was ordered to cross the river to reconnoitre a new site for the field guns.

Since the opening of the Class 9 bridge DAVID the previous evening, all the vehicles belonging to the six battalions over the river had crossed the Seine. Towards the end of the morning there was a lull in the traffic going across and everything was relatively quiet. It was during this lull that the bridging area came under long-range artillery fire from the Germans. (After the battle, Major Concannon found these guns that had bombarded the river, left abandoned in their positions several miles inland. They were discovered to be captured Russian howitzers of about 6in (152mm) calibre.)

The shells fell indiscriminately around the bridging site, with one chance shot inflicting a direct hit on the folding boat bridge. As fate would have it, there was a dispatch rider crossing the river and he happened to be in the very spot that the shell struck. He was blown to smithereens and a section of the bridge was destroyed. An ambulance, following thirty yards behind, managed to stop just before it reached the gaping hole in the road.

When Major Concannon and his party arrived at the recently damaged bridge, he was told that there would be a long wait before they could cross. Concannon began chatting to the Royal Engineer officer in charge, to while away the time:

Someone came up to us and said that there was an interesting house nearby that he thought we might like to see. Out of curiosity we went and had a look. It turned out to be a very sumptuously furnished brothel. I remember there were some very peculiar looking chairs there, the use of which we could only guess at. Fortunately for us, or unfortunately rather, there was nobody in the house, they had all taken refuge somewhere else in the town.

By the time Concannon had rejoined his survey party at the water's edge, a Class 9 raft had been brought into operation to ferry vehicles over the river. Within thirty minutes the gunners were once again on their way. They found their regiment's CO talking with Brigadier Mole at 129 Brigade's headquarters. Lieutenant-Colonel Bishell told them to press on into the forest to find out the latest news from the 4th Somersets, who should by then have reached Bois Jérôme. This they did and soon reached the Somersets' regimental aid post, where they were told of the fighting in progress up ahead. A further move of a few hundred yards brought them much closer to the sounds of battle.

The two jeeps pulled off the track and backed into the thick undergrowth. Major Concannon had decided to go the remainder of the way to the Somersets' HQ on foot. He did not get far, for almost immediately, just as the rest of the group had settled down for a chat, a German 20mm anti-aircraft cannon started firing down the track from very close range. Small shells exploded in the trees all around, wounding the signals officer, Lieutenant Bill Stockton. The enemy gun was located only a hundred yards away in a small glade, close by a set of cross tracks, and was sighted to fire along each of the rides converging at that point. It had the whole area covered, trapping the two jeeps in the undergrowth so they were unable to move forwards again.

It was an unfortunate coincidence, but at that very moment there was another survey party from the Royal Artillery performing its own reconnaissance in the Forest of Vernon. It was led by Major Sir John Backhouse, second-in-command of the 179th Field Regiment, supporting 214 Brigade. He, too, was in the same section of woods looking for new sites for his guns and was driving slowly towards the set of cross tracks. Before he could be warned of the impending danger, the German gun opened fire on his scout car. Sir John was hit in the head and collapsed to the ground as the small shells exploded all around the car. Concannon and his party managed to get the wounded major to cover, but he was in a bad way. He died later that day.

The troublesome enemy gun continued to interfere with any signs of movement along the tracks. A short time later a carrier from the Somersets was hit and burst into flames. Then, to the amazement of the watching gunners, a jeep from another unit drove slowly towards the enemy gun with the occupants holding up their hands in surrender!

By this time Major Concannon was beginning to get a little irritated with his predicament. He was anxious to get on with his job, but was trapped. The gun was in a very strong position, although it was completely surrounded. Its crew were determined to fight to the last and showed no signs of surrendering.

It did cross my mind to organise a little sortie to try to capture the enemy gun with the five men left in my party. I thought that with all the bombs and grenades in our jeeps we could knock the gun out, but I then thought better of it, deciding that my first priority was to get the regiment's new positions sorted out, so that the advance could continue. Our immediate problem was how to get out of the thick undergrowth.

If the jeeps could not go forwards because of the enemy, then Concannon felt the only course left was to go backwards. His battle wagon carried all sorts of equipment in anticipation of just such an eventuality. There were axes, saws, cold chisels and a host of tools and weapons. The gunners decided to play at lumberjacks and chopped a path through the foliage for the jeep to reverse to safety.

Concannon later revisited the site in the woods where the action had taken place and found the German 20mm cannon still in position after it had finally been knocked out by the Somersets:

Lying close by the gun was the four-man detachment; all had been killed at their posts. Around the site were great piles of empty shell cases, serving as a testimony to the terrific fire they had put down and which had caused us such trouble. They were very brave men sticking to their task as they did, even though they were hopelessly outnumbered and surrounded on all sides.

Whilst 214 Brigade and the 4th Somersets had been coping with the counter-attack by Battle Group Schrader, the other two battalions of 129 Brigade (4th and 5th Wiltshires) were continuing their expansion of the bridgehead. The 5th Wiltshires were trying to advance to the south-eastern edge of the Forest of Vernon, along the Gasny road. Progress was slow; a mobile 37mm gun was giving them problems. Twice the advance was halted by this weapon. Each time a patrol was sent forward to locate the gun and then an artillery concentration was put down on the spot. However, when the carrier platoon moved in to follow up the barrage, the enemy gun had withdrawn. It took all morning to cover the 2,000 yards (1,828m) to the edge of the woods. Here the two leading companies were told to dig in with their trenches overlooking the flat open country towards the village of La Chapelle St Ouen, about a mile and a half away. The battalion HQ was situated in the forest, 500 yards (457m) to the rear, with 'C' Company forming a forward-facing defensive arc around it. In this commanding position, protecting the approaches from the south-east, the battalion spent the remainder of the day. Thomas was not sure where the Germans would strike next. He ordered the advance to halt until the counter-attack against the north and eastern parts of the bridgehead was contained and the enemy's intentions were made clear.

To the right of the bridging sites, the high ground that lined the river had been assigned to the 4th Wiltshires to clear. Since early morning they had been continuing their sweep along the cliffs and up the Seine valley, with the village of Giverny as their objective. The battalion moved with two companies up on the ridge and two along the bottom next to the river. For the first few hours they enjoyed an easy time. There was no enemy opposition, but there was an abundance of delicious apples in the orchards that dotted the hillside on the approaches to Giverny and the troops ate their fill. With the village in sight, 'C' Company up on the hilltop was ordered to secure the high ground behind Giverny as a prelude to 'D' Company's attack along the road.

Commanding 'C' Company up on that hill was Major 'Dim' Robbins. Colonel Luce had told him to outflank the village and give supporting fire to the main attack:

To my interest and horror, I saw a long line of German soldiers marching along the road in good order intent on reinforcing the village from the far end. I remember thinking to myself that with all those in the place it was going to be a good fight. Then, I know I did wrong, I immediately ordered my men to open fire, even though the range was rather long. We hit a few, but most of them vanished into the houses. It was a bad move, we all knew how difficult a job it was to fight anyone out of a village.

'C' Company's firing from the ridge had caught the enemy by surprise; the strong-points along the road on the edge of Giverny were embarrassed to find their positions enfiladed from the right flank. At the same time, 'D' Company rushed the village along the flat road, supported by armoured cars. It was unsuccessful; the attack was beaten off and one of the armoured cars' troop commanders was shot dead. The battalion waited whilst an artillery barrage was put down on the enemy strong-points.

During the afternoon, the 4th Wiltshires were joined by a troop of Cromwell tanks, together with their squadron commander, from the 15th/19th Royal Hussars. The troop's Challenger tank was left at the ferry site, having failed to start. Whilst the squadron commander put down a smoke-screen, the Cromwells slowly ground their way up the steep hill in bottom gear to join 'C' Company on the top, overlooking the village. They added their firepower to that of the battalion and another infantry attack on Giverny was put in along the main road, supported by the squadron commander's tank. This was a little more successful than the previous one and a foothold was gained amongst the houses on the edge of the village. By this time, the light was beginning to fade and it was getting too dark to start the difficult task of clearing all the houses and buildings of the enemy. Colonel Luce called a halt to the proceedings and set his battalion to consolidate their small gains until morning.

Fortunately, this side of the bridgehead had not been confronted by the counter-attacking Battle Group Schrader; the opposition consisted of those of the enemy who had been guarding this section of the river for the past week. As such, the 4th Wiltshires were able to advance against these lesser troops further than any other battalion that day.

To almost all the men of the 4th Wiltshires, Giverny was just one of the scores of villages of France that had to be taken by force. This 'first' village of Normandy, situated alongside the confluence of the Seine and the Epte, marked the border of the Duchy with that of the Ile-de-France. However, to Lieutenant-Colonel Ted Luce there was a much greater significance about the place. His wife was something of an artist and, to all those who love art, the name of Giverny will forever be associated with Claude Monet.

Monet had chosen a home in the hillside village overlooking the Seine in 1883 and it was here, at the rear of his house, that he made his water garden. Before his death, just eighteen years earlier in 1926, he had painted that garden countless times. Those bright canvases, showing the water lilies and the little Japanese bridge, were familiar to the whole world. Nevertheless, war has scant respect for art. The liberating army sweeping up the Seine valley was on the verge of brushing against this idyllic scene. The axis for the next day's advance was along the railway line that separated Monet's house and the water garden. Tomorrow, Luce would get to see those water lilies, should those delicate flowers survive the arrival of the Wessexmen.

Much earlier that day, back in Vernon, the folding boat bridge DAVID had come under shell fire. The direct hit on the bridge had destroyed two floating bays, with the damaged boats being left suspended from the shattered roadbearers. Considerable difficulty was experienced in the attempts to discard the broken portion. It was found to be impossible to remove all the damaged boats, although one was eventually dropped off, for the weight of the raft connectors made it extremely tricky to disconnect the roadbearers. Explosives could not be used because of the risk to other good boats. Oxy-acetylene cutting flame was the only answer, but it was a long job; DAVID was closed for almost two hours.

The shells that had smashed the 43rd Division's Class 9 bridge had also caused trouble for the 7th Army Troops Royal Engineers, who were constructing the first Bailey. All of the hits had been on the Vernonnet side of the river. The damage done to the area was considerable. The bridging company had suffered around fifteen casualties, with nine of the thirty men from the Pioneer Corps lost. Two bulldozers, in the process of carving a road through the back gardens of the houses lining the approach to the old bridge, were knocked out and a lorry loaded with bridging equipment was reduced to a burning hulk. For a moment, all work on the far side came to an abrupt halt.

Lieutenant-Colonel Tom Lloyd was soon on the scene to explain to his men just how much depended on the bridge and how vital it was that work be quickly resumed. The sappers did not need an elaborate pep talk. Taking a lead from their company commander, a huge person, twice the size of an ordinary man, they were soon back at work. He wasn't worrying, so why should they? Lloyd came away with the odd impression that they were still quite enjoying the job.

The early completion of the bridge was of paramount importance. XXX Corps' chief engineer, Brigadier Davey, had told Lloyd that the corps' armour was at that very moment closing on the river at full speed, anxious to take advantage of the golden opportunity now presenting itself for a dash across northern France against weak opposition. Everything depended on just how quickly the bridge could be made ready and the bridgehead secured. Lloyd told the brigadier to have a column of tanks lined up in Vernon along the approaches to the bridge by 1800 hours. The presence of rows of armour, in full view of the sappers, would help to keep them convinced of the urgency of their task.

The flurry of shells that had damaged the bridging sites turned out to be the enemy's final goodbye to the Seine. The expansion of the lodgement area had over-run the last active German battery in the area. The enemy had abandoned what was left of the artillery; they no longer had any ammunition available, nor transport to move the guns. The waterfront of Vernon was now given over to the relatively peaceful pursuit of bridge-building. The construction of the Bailey was coming along fine, or so Tom Lloyd thought.

The bridge, being built out from both banks, was gradually taking shape, closing on a final small gap that would inevitably occur in the middle. This gap would be breached by pushing forward the landing bays from each side of the river, which had already been placed on rollers in preparation for the move. When these bays were finally in position, they would be jacked up and the rollers removed. The landing bays would then be set down on prepared foundations. During the morning, with the bridge about half completed, the remaining gap was measured with a graduated cable. Lloyd calculated from this that the final small gap in the middle would be about four feet (1.2m). This could be closed by moving just the landing bay on the far side of the river. To save half-an-hour, he ordered the nearside landing bay to be taken off its rollers and put down in position. Later in the afternoon, the last floating bay was towed into the bridge and connected up. The final gap was measured and found to be six feet (1.8m). Lloyd's mental arithmetic earlier in the day had been somewhat wide of the mark: 'The chief engineer happened along just then. He asked whether everything was all right. "Fine," I replied, but I was thinking "damnation". That six-foot gap looked to me like six miles for the moment.'

Tom Lloyd was, however, a bridging expert. Experience had taught him to be prepared for any vagaries in the width of a river. He had taken the precaution of making the two landing bays ten feet (3m) longer than they needed to be. By lengthening one of them and putting the bays on rollers once again, the sappers soon closed the gap.

This final closing of the gap was something of an anticlimax. Although looking complete, there was still much work to be done on the Bailey. Ramps had to be placed at both ends, footwalks constructed, decking laid and, most importantly, the strain on the pontoon's anchor cables had to be equalised, so as to bring the bridge into a straight line in the fast-flowing river. All this work came at a time when the men were all but exhausted.

Then came the moment for the first vehicle to cross. At 1745 a bulldozer went over to continue work on the far exits from the river. Three-quarters of an hour later the bridge was brought into use, but still only for the engineers' trucks. Tipping lorries, filled with rubble and stone, lumbered across to lay a hard base for the road up into Vernonnet. Then, at last, came the first of the tanks. At 1930 on 27 August, just over forty-eight hours after the initial assault, the first 40-ton Bailey over the River Seine was opened. GOLIATH was ready for business. The 684ft (208m) bridge had taken 500 engineers 28 hours to construct. The human cost: twenty men killed or injured.

With two bridges open, the third of the division's brigades, 130 Brigade, speeded up its move into the lodgement area. Since earlier that morning the brigade had been moving slowly across the smaller Class 9 bridge. Now the final three battalions of the division and all their vehicles and guns poured over both bridges. With them came the tanks of the 8th Armoured Brigade. They crossed to join their lead regiment, the 4th/7th Royal Dragoon Guards, to be ready for the 43rd Division's big push inland the next day as all nine of Thomas's battalions moved to the bridgehead's final objectives.

By the evening it looked to Thomas as though his division had blunted the German counter-attack against the northern and eastern parts of the lodgement. Latest reports from his two brigade commanders showed that the enemy had been halted and had probably started to withdraw. Patrols from the various battalions showed that in most cases there were no longer any hostile troops in front of them. Both brigades had stopped their advance to deal with the counter-attack and by early evening five of the six battalions had dug in for the night; the sixth, however, was still on the offensive.

Colonel Lipscombe's 4th Somersets had been joined by tanks. Having dealt with the enemy attack to his rear, he was determined to press on and secure his original objective, the village of Bois Jérôme. By the time the armour was in position for the assault, the light had faded considerably. Lipscombe dismissed the leading company commander's objection that it was too dark to use tank support effectively and ordered 'A' Company to secure a lodgement in the village.

The attack was put in from due west of Bois Jérôme. The noise was deafening as the tanks opened up with their main armament, supported by their hull-mounted machine-guns. Artillery joined in and a barrage of fire fell on the quiet unsuspecting hamlet. Once again the whole forest echoed to the sound of battle. Then 'A' Company went in. The attack was a formality; there was no opposition. Patrols carried on to the northern end of the village and found it clear; the enemy had gone.

When the battalion had at last secured Bois Jérôme, it was quite dark. The shell fire had set light to a few houses and had caused casualties to some civilians sheltering in the village. Corporal Hitchcock was a member of 'A' Company, which was doing the clearing up:

There was a complete row of houses on fire and I think some people were trapped inside. I could hear kiddies crying. Our job was to make sure there were no Germans hiding in Bois Jérôme and we began to search every building. I remember one house had a chink of light showing in the darkness. It was to the left of a large manor with a walled garden (there were beautiful pears on the trees gowing against the wall and we had our fill of them the next day). Two of us crept towards the door, listened and then pushed it carefully open, grenades at the ready. Inside we were confronted by four women. One had suffered a bullet wound in her thigh from a stray shot fired during the bombardment. Soon we were joined by others of my platoon and you can imagine the ribald comments that were bandied about as we attended to the unfortunate woman's wound. Other men began to poke around, looking all over the house. All of a sudden, a broad Somerset voice called out from upstairs that there was a Jerry under the bed, to which one wit replied that he also had one under his bed at home! In fact there was a German hiding upstairs, but we soon had him out, tied his hands and sent him back to company HQ. I believe he was the only prisoner taken in Bois Jérôme.

With the village in safe hands, the 4th Somersets, too, dug in for the night. It was to be a very uncomfortable night, for around midnight there was a terrific thunderstorm with torrential rain. By morning, the troops in the slit trenches were up to their waists in water.

Away to the left on the Gisors road, the situation had been stable for most of the afternoon. The 1st Worcestershires had halted the attack by Battle Group Schrader and the Tiger was content to remain where it was in the middle of the road. Both sides spent the remainder of the daylight hours firing wildly into the trees in an attempt to dissuade any further movement by their opponents. In this they were both successful, for neither side moved forward again that day. At about 2000 hours, the enemy tank put down a smoke-screen and withdrew up the road, leaving the infantry where they were.

A little later, the battalion's commanding officer called an 'O' group meeting in a small hut by the side of the road to decide on a patrol programme for the rest of the night. In the darkness, the company commanders all gathered around the light of a single torch, trying to make out their positions from the various maps. It was at this moment, with all the battalion's senior officers most vulnerable, confined as they were in a very small space, that they were subjected to another attack. Somebody disturbed a hornets' nest in the roof and the night was filled with hundreds of buzzing insects. In a moment the hut had cleared. With arms flailing, the officers all desperately beat the space around their heads with their mapboards, the air turning blue with their cursing. Scattering in all directions, they repelled this second attack of the day, fortunately without further serious casualties.

As night fell, the question of sending out patrols was tackled by the infantry battalions. In perfect circumstances, before a patrol is normally sent out the men would be thoroughly briefed, rested and fed. On this occasion, as on many similar occasions in the fierce fighting that had occurred, it was not possible. The Worcestershires had been in action the whole of the day and everyone was exhausted. Nevertheless, patrols had to go out to find out just what the enemy were doing. That night it fell to a very junior lieutenant to lead one such patrol up onto the hill, to see if the enemy were still in a small 'summer-house' on top. Watching the young officer receiving his orders was Major Jackie Goldsmid of the 4th/7th Royal Dragoon Guards:

> None of the preparation had been done before the patrol and this poor little bugger looked absolutely worn out. I remember thinking to myself that it would not be much good sending him out. As a spectator, it was awful to see this poor chap go off up that hill towards the enemy in pitch darkness. A while later the patrol came back. They had no information to offer, explaining they had got lost. The lieutenant was rather shamefaced about it, but nothing was said. I think by that time the commanding officer had gone to bed.

No one knew if enemy troops were still on the hill, or if they had followed the Tiger's example and withdrawn. What was known, however, was that they were still further up the road, because weaving streams of tracer continued to be fired down the valley from time to time throughout the night – but most of the Worcestershires were beyond caring, so deep was their sleep.

Major Algy Grubb had found the day quite stimulating. He looked upon the action as a 'gentleman's battle'. Although there had been, as he admits, 'a great deal of stuff flying about', most of it was small arms:

> It may now seem rather an incomprehensible thing to say, but it could be great fun. What was really tiresome was when the shells came; then you had no chance. Tanks and things made it a hell of a bloody game, but a little gentleman's war was a great deal of fun. At that time, after the experience we had been through, one was attuned to it, inoculated against it. You really were, you became a little elated, unbalanced even.
>
> On reflection, it appears odd that you could enjoy such a thing, but it is an example of an extraordinary reaction of the body that I think is largely due to the generation of adrenalin. In moments of intense danger, I believe if one is made that way, and somehow I was, one became elated to such an extent that it bordered on insanity. When it was all over, there was total collapse. On one occasion I was out for twenty-four hours; nobody could

wake me. At Mont Pinçon, we started out with eighty-six men and ended with just five. I was mad with elation upon something that I felt was impossible. It also happened here on the Seine. When it was all over, I collapsed into a very small slit trench and went completely out. In fact, I nearly drowned. A tremendous thunderstorm during the night had filled my trench with water and when I came to the next morning it was just below my nose. I had no idea it had been raining! I was carrying a picture of my girlfriend (now wife) in my blue morocco wallet at the time. I still have it, all blue from the water.

When they had left England just two months earlier, none of the division, not even in their blackest nightmares, could have dreamed of what lay ahead. Now in August, on the Seine, those who had survived Normandy were completely different people inside. All of them had lost very dear friends. Replacements had arrived and been killed before their names were known. The scale of the slaughter left no man in any doubt that the day would surely dawn when he too would be lying beneath one of the stark white crosses that seemed to line every road and country lane. So it was on the road to Gisors. Of the 553 men belonging to the Worcestershires who set out that morning, 26 of them were dead and 65 others wounded. All this in an action which, when taken in the context of the earlier fighting, was no more than a skirmish. In just two short months, the battalion, which had begun the campaign so full of friends, had become a battalion full of strangers. The survivors were all left with a fatalistic view of their future.

Situation at 2100 Hours Sunday 27 August
The Wessex Division had successfully blunted the counter-attack by Battle Group Schrader. In doing so, it had suffered only relatively slight casualties and there had been no loss of ground to the enemy. With most of his division now across the river and established, Thomas had the battle virtually won.

Chapter 17

Bridgehead Secured

Monday 28 August was another dry, sunny day, in stark contrast to the thunderstorm and heavy rain of the night before. Thomas was by that time confident that his bridgehead was secure. All of the reports from the previous night's patrols showed that the enemy was pulling out. The advance inland was set to continue.

With the arrival of 130 Brigade and the remainder of the 8th Armoured Brigade into the lodgement area, Thomas had ample troops available to secure all of his final objectives. He planned that by the end of the day he would control a semicircle four and a half miles (7km) deep, centred on the bridges at Vernonnet. All of his infantry battalions were to advance, with the exception of the 1st Worcestershires. (After the mauling they had received the day before, they were given the job of taking over Pressagny l'Orgueilleux from the 5th Cornwalls and holding the left flank.)

130 Brigade was ordered to complete the task given the day before to the Worcestershires, that of the capture of the village of Tilly, and then to move on to La Queue d'Haye; 129 Brigade was to continue along its axis of the previous day, whilst 214 Brigade, less the 1st Worcestershires, cleared the northern part of the Forest of Vernon, with the 5th Cornwalls given the task of capturing Panilleuse.

During the night, there had been a non-stop stream of traffic rumbling across the two newly built bridges. The third bridge, another Class 40 Bailey, should have been started at first light, although the XXX Corps' chief engineer seemed to think that there was no hurry about it. The sappers reserved for the task of construction were the 15th (Kent) GHQ Troops Royal Engineers, commanded by Colonel Fayle. This was to be their third task in the operation, having already manned the assault boats and built and operated the tank ferry. An hour after these troops had bedded down for the night, they were rudely awakened from their sleep and Fayle was told that the job had suddenly become urgent. The bridge had now to be ready for 1200 hours on Tuesday 29 August. Fayle and his men had just thirty-six hours to build this 736-foot (223m) Bailey, codenamed SAUL.

Soon after dawn, in the depths of the Forest of Vernon, the 7th Somerset Light Infantry sent a reconnaissance patrol to the site of 'A' Company's disappearance the day before. As expected, there was no sign of them. During the patrol, only two Germans were seen; the whole area looked to have been given up by the enemy.

Later in the day, the battalion advanced with the aid of some tanks of the Sherwood Rangers (part of 8th Armoured Brigade) and secured all its original objectives. There was no more enemy interference in the forest. Lieutenant-Colonel Nichol then made a thorough examination of the luckless 'A' Company's final positions.

There were some casualties found around the set of cross tracks: three dead and three injured, all belonging to the Somersets. Civilians from a nearby farmhouse reported seeing about fifty or sixty prisoners being taken away by the Germans. It seemed that what had probably happened was that the two platoons belonging to 'A' Company had arrived at the cross tracks and had been placed in the woods to cover the area, but were attacked by Battle Group Schrader before they could establish themselves adequately. The forest here was particularly dense, with visibility down to just a few yards. Unfortunately the separation between the two platoons was about thirty yards (27m), much too wide, given the circumstances, to be covered by defensive fire.

A German heavy machine-gun, sited by the farmhouse on the right, had opened up with accurate fire in support of the attack on the Somersets. The main body of the enemy had then made for the gap between the two Wessex platoons and quickly broke through to the rear. Within minutes 'A' Company was surrounded, pinned down by fire from all directions. Completely overwhelmed, the company had surrendered. It was a tragedy for the battalion, caused partly by bad luck (being caught by a large body of attacking infantry whilst unprepared) and partly by the company commander's lack of battle experience in placing his troops. It also turned out to be a tragedy for Colonel Nichol.

When Thomas heard the news of this he was furious. The loss of a complete company, given up with only minimal casualties and at a time of such dire infantry shortages, was an unpardonable sin. The whole area lacked the debris of a hard-fought battle; the surrender seemed too soon, too easy. To Thomas it was inexcusable. His reaction was true to form and, living up to his nickname of 'the butcher', he sacked Nichol. Despite strong protests by Brigadier Essame, Thomas was adamant. Lieutenant-Colonel Nichol DSO was posted to the staff of XXX Corps HQ.

It was a particularly harsh decision by General Thomas, especially if, as the evidence suggests, it was on his insistence that the original move to that map reference was made. Nevertheless, as battalion commander, it was

Nichol who had to take the blame. This was most unfortunate, for Nichol was a very good soldier. His citation for his DSO won in the earlier fighting states: '... he showed outstanding personal courage and capacity to command in the face of heavy resistance'. The battalion was sad to lose him in such wretched circumstances, but, as one participant at Vernon recalls: 'Thomas was a shit. He would do anything to save his own neck.'

The enemy's resistance to the 43rd Division's expansion of the bridgehead that Monday was spasmodic. The German 49th Division had shot its bolt. With the demise of the counter-attack by Battle Group Schrader, opposition began to fade away; not completely though, for there was still a little more blood to be shed before Thomas could signal 'bridgehead captured' to his corps commander.

From their slit trenches on the edge of a wood, the 5th Wiltshires looked out across the flat cornfields towards the village of La Chapelle St Ouen, a mile and a half away. The capture of the village was the battalion's objective for that day. At the same time, the 4th Somersets were to capture the neighbouring village of Haricourt, a mile to the left.

During the previous night, Sergeant Norman Smith of 'D' Company was told to take a reconnaissance patrol out towards the village to try to determine how many of the enemy were there. He was told that there were no other patrols out that night, so passwords would not be necessary:

I had about six men with me and we set off across the open fields in pouring rain. There was some enemy fire, just mortars and small arms, being directed at our lines, but it was quite random and aimed at nothing in particular. A little later, as we approached the village, a pom-pom gun opened up, sending a stream of small shells towards the woods behind us. After a short while it stopped. Then a few minutes later another gun opened up away to the left. Soon this too stopped, only to be followed after a short pause by another pom-pom a few hundred yards away.

Closer inspection by the patrol found that there was just a single anti-aircraft gun mounted on a horse-drawn trailer. This was being ridden up and down the road, firing at random, to give the impression of there being a number of guns guarding the village. Nothing more of the enemy could be seen.

The patrol over, Smith and his men made their way back towards the Wiltshires' lines. Stumbling across the muddy fields in torrential rain, the patrol was surprised to find itself approached by a shadowy group of figures heading its way. Both parties saw each other at the same moment and dropped smartly to the ground. Lying there in the thick mud, Smith was not sure what to do next. He was convinced it must be an enemy patrol, because no other patrols were supposed to be out that night, and yet he was still reluctant to be the first to open fire. The other group just lay there motionless, barely thirty yards away. Smith decided to take a chance and challenged them in English; there was no reply. He shouted again; still there was silence. By this time, he was sure they were German. One more try and then he would open fire. For a third time, he shouted as loud as he could above the noise of the pouring rain, his voice almost faltering as he tensed himself ready to act. This time, there was a reply. An accusing, 'Who are you?' came out of the stormy night. It was a patrol from the 8th Middlesex, the division's heavy machine-gun battalion. They were reconnoitring the ground in preparation for the next day's attack. Smith was so relieved and yet angry too: the mix-up could have proved fatal.

The next morning the attack on La Chapelle St Ouen was made. It was a set-piece assault. 'B' and 'D' Companies of the 5th Wiltshires attacked across the flat cornfields. They advanced in line abreast, one single wave of no more than a hundred men. There was no cover, for once the infantry had left the shelter of the forest, they passed into open view. In support, an artillery barrage was laid down by the 94th Field Regiment, and firing over the heads of the Wiltshires were the heavy machine-guns and mortars of the 8th Middlesex. Away to the right, along the road from Vernonnet to Gasny, a troop of Sherman tanks from the 13th/18th Hussars lent weight to the attack.

'B' Company was on the right, nearest to the road, and 'D' Company on the left. Sergeant Smith of 'D' Company remembers the attack as being a simple affair. Some derisory fire was aimed at the Wiltshires, but on the whole there was almost negligible resistance. The company walked across the fields and entered the village without loss. However, just a few hundred yards away from him, 'B' Company had a nasty experience.

There was no sign of the enemy as the leading platoon of the right-hand company came to within a hundred yards of the village. Then, suddenly, all three section commanders were hit. They were dead before they touched the ground. The company had come under concentrated machine-gun fire from very short range. The bullets ripped through the advancing troops like a scythe. In an instant, the whole company had dropped to the ground, each man pressing himself into the cornfield's coarse stubble in an attempt to become invisible. Lying there in the open, more men were hit and the casualties quickly began to mount.

The enemy fire had come from some stacks of corn standing innocently in front of the village. Once located, the Wiltshires brought down swift retribution on the unfortunate German defenders. The 2in (50mm) mortars belonging to the company opened up and were soon joined by direct fire from the Hussars' Sherman tanks. At the same time, the infantry jumped up and rushed the demoralised enemy. In a very short while, both companies had entered the village. The Germans surrendered en masse. By the time La Chapelle St Ouen was finally cleared, 160 prisoners had been taken. The enemy troops defending the village were of low calibre, each looking for the earliest opportunity to lay down his arms. They never had any real intention of putting up a fight, being resigned to just letting off a few rounds and then throwing up their hands in subjugation. To them, the loss of the village was a foregone conclusion; it was inevitable. Their task was merely a delaying tactic in the face of the inexorable Allied tide sweeping over France towards Germany. Sadly for the ten dead Wiltshiremen, lying silently on the bloodstained earth out on the empty cornfields, the enemy's futile gesture had cost them their lives.

'The enemy troops that we captured that day all seemed to be Polish,' remembers Norman Smith.

They had been forced into the Germany army and had no stomach for the fighting. Their officers were no better. Apparently, when we started to put our attack in, the officers jumped on motorbikes and into small Opel cars and escaped from the rear of the village. Left on their own, the Poles soon packed it in. There was only slight damage done to the village, although some cattle were killed by the machine-gun fire from the 8th Middlesex. The French civilians were happy to see us, all except the farmers; they were hopping mad about their dead cows.

Smith could not understand what all the fuss was about. He suggested that they should get a butcher to clean up the meat and eat it. The farmers were furious; they would have nothing to do with that idea. At one point Smith thought they were going to attack him. Fortunately, 'B' Company had its own butcher and he had no compunction about preparing the dead cattle. He saw to it that at least his company had some fresh meat.

Throughout the whole of the bridgehead, the advance inland that day proceeded according to Thomas's plan. Formal attacks took place against a succession of villages and all were taken without any serious casualties.

The village of Haricourt, on the left of the 5th Wiltshires, was carried by the 4th Somerset Light Infantry around noon. The third battalion from 129 Brigade was also in action as Ted Luce's 4th Wiltshires took Monet's village of Giverny without further damage. Luce himself was later lodged in the great man's house and it was rumoured that the artist's widow gave him one of Monet's brushes as a souvenir.

To the north, 130 Brigade attacked the villages on both sides of the Gisors road. The 4th Dorsets cleared the high ground that had caused so much trouble to the Worcestershires the day before, leaving the 5th Dorsets to pass through and capture the villages of La Queue d'Haye and Heubécourt. On their left, the 7th Hampshires had captured Tilly by around 1600 hours, but not without some awkward moments in the woods outside the village, caused by remnants of Battle Group Schrader.

Following closely behind the Hampshires into Tilly was a carrier from 220 Battery of 112 Field Regiment Royal Artillery. At its controls was Bombardier R. Barber:

> I remember our party had the daylights scared out of us. As we came round a bend in the road leading up from the river, there before us was a Tiger tank. Fortunately this had already been knocked out (by the Worcestershires) and we motored on into the recently captured Tilly. There were still fires burning in the village and we pulled into the square just in time to witness the local fire brigade going into action. The firemen all seemed to be dressed in various braided uniforms and were manhandling an old hand-operated fire engine. It looked very amusing, like something out of a Chaplin film, but they were behaving very bravely indeed for there were still some Germans around, although most had been captured or had fled. From the church tower I could see long lines of the enemy pulling out from the area.

Around mid-afternoon, on the left of the bridgehead, the 5th Cornwalls handed over the control of Pressagny l'Orgueilleux to the tired Worcestershires and set out south-east through the forest to Panilleuse. The 7th Somersets had already reached their final objective at the edge of the woods when Taylor took his men past them and out into the open. Below them, in the late afternoon's pale sunshine, lay the division's last objective: Panilleuse. It was 1700 hours.

The taking of Panilleuse was a perfectly executed set-piece infantry attack. Supported by tanks of the Sherwood Rangers and the artillery of 179 Field Regiment, the Cornishmen swept down into the village. They attacked with such determination that one officer and four privates were injured as they dashed through their own shellfire to get at the enemy. A few Germans were killed in their slit trenches on the outskirts of the village, but the majority of the enemy took flight. The process of finally clearing the village of the last of the German stragglers was considerably impeded by the welcome of the French population, as Colonel Taylor recalls:

> They welcomed our men with great enthusiasm, thrusting flowers on them, giving them wine to drink and kissing the somewhat embarrassed soldiers. One Frenchman, who, in a glorious state of intoxication, kept roaring the 'Marseillaise' and throwing his arms around the necks of the officers, had to be put under restraint. The French said that our attack had driven out about eighty of the enemy who fled up the road with more haste than dignity. By the light of the burning buildings the position was consolidated.

As darkness fell, the commander of the last battalion in action that day radioed a message back to brigade HQ: 'Panilleuse captured'. The battle for the Seine bridgehead was over.

Major-General Thomas and his division had completed the orders given to them just seven days previously by the corps commander. The 43rd Division had forced a crossing of the River Seine at Vernon, covered the construction of three bridges and formed a bridgehead of sufficient depth to allow passage through of the remainder of the corps. Thomas's 'epic operation' was complete.

That afternoon control of the bridges at Vernon passed to XXX Corps, which was assembling just outside the town. The stage could now be given over to the corps to act as spearhead for the whole Twenty-First Army Group, as the advance continued towards Germany.

Bibliography

Blumenson, M. *Breakout and Pursuit* (Washington, 1961)

Ellis, F. *Victory in the West* (HMSO, London, 1962)

Essame, H. *The 43rd Division at War 1944–1945* (Clowes, London, 1952)

Gill, R. and Groves, J. *Club Route in Europe* (Hannover, 1946)

Godfrey, E.G. *The History of the Duke of Cornwall's Light Infantry 1939–1945* (Gale & Polden, London, 1946)

Hartwell, G.R., Pack, G.R. and Edwards, M.A. *The Story of the 5th Battalion The Dorsetshire Regiment in North West Europe 23rd June 1944 to 5th May 1945* (Henry Ling Printers, Dorchester, 1946)

Horrocks, B. *Corps Commander* (Sidgwick & Jackson, London, 1977)

Lipscombe, C.G. *History of 4th Battalion Somerset Light Infantry (Prince Albert's) in the Campaign in N.W. Europe June 1944–May 1945* (E. Goodman, Phoenix Press, 1945)

Lloyd, T. *The Seine! The Seine!* (Sifton Praed, London, 1946)

McMath, J.S. *The Fifth Battalion The Wiltshire Regiment in NW Europe, June 1944–May 1945* (Whitefriars Press, London, 1946)

Meredith, J.L.J. *The Story of the Seventh Battalion Somerset Light Infantry*

Montgomery, B.L. *Normandy to the Baltic* (Hutchinson, London, 1947)

Parsons, A.D., Robbins, D.I.M. and Gilson, D.C. *The Maroon Square: A History of the 4th Battalion the Wiltshire Regiment in NW Europe* (Franey Co. Ltd, London, 1948)

Watkins, G.J.B. *From Normandy to the Weser. The War History of the 4th Battalion The Dorset Regiment. June 1944–May 1945* (Henry Ling Printers, Dorchester, 1946)

Watson, D.Y. *First Battalion Worcestershire Regiment in North West Europe*

Appendix 1

During the advance to the River Seine, all the vehicles belonging to the 43rd Division and the supporting arms were separated into three groups. The composition of these groups was dependent on the point at which they were introduced into the battle. In order to demonstrate the complexity of an infantry division in action, the make-up of these groups is listed, together with the number of vehicles they contained:

Group One (assault group)

43rd Reconnaissance Regiment (less one squadron)	105 vehicles
4th Battalion Wiltshire Regiment	130 vehicles
94th Field Regiment Royal Artillery	135 vehicles
234 Anti-Tank Battery	35 vehicles
129 Infantry Brigade Tactical HQ	12 vehicles
'A' and 'D' Companies 8th Middlesex Regiment	85 vehicles
260 Field Company Royal Engineers	25 vehicles
4th Battalion Somerset Light Infantry	90 vehicles
129 Infantry Brigade Main HQ	45 vehicles
43rd Division Tactical HQ	60 vehicles
129 Field Ambulance	35 vehicles
360 Light Anti-Aircraft Regiment Royal Artillery	25 vehicles
235 Anti-Tank Battery Royal Artillery	35 vehicles
5th Battalion Wiltshire Regiment	90 vehicles
1st Battalion Worcestershire Regiment	90 vehicles
Royal Engineers Group	210 vehicles
129 Infantry Brigade 'A' Echelon vehicles	230 vehicles

Total 1437 Vehicles

Group Two

Royal Artillery Reconnaissance Parties	90 vehicles
'A' Squadron 43rd Reconnaissance Regiment	50 vehicles
71st Light Anti-Aircraft Regiment R.A.	50 vehicles
121st Medium Regiment Royal Artillery	119 vehicles
179th Field Regiment Royal Artillery	100 vehicles
112th Field Regiment Royal Artillery	100 vehicles

4th/7th Dragoon Guards	100 vehicles
5th Duke of Cornwall's Light Infantry	90 vehicles
7th Somerset Light Infantry	90 vehicles
'B' Company 8th Middlesex Regiment	34 vehicles
334 Anti-Tank Battery Royal Artillery	40 vehicles
214 Infantry Brigade H.Q.	40 vehicles
43rd Division Main H.Q.	80 vehicles
Number 2 Group Royal Engineers	444 vehicles
214th Field Ambulance	30 vehicles
Number 2 Group Royal Army Service Corps	220 vehicles

Total 1677 Vehicles

Group Three

'C' Company 8th Middlesex Regiment	34 vehicles
130th Field Ambulance	30 vehicles
5th Battalion Dorset Regiment	90 vehicles
4th Battalion Dorset Regiment	90 vehicles
7th Battalion Hampshire Regiment	90 vehicles
130 Infantry Brigade HQ	40 vehicles
43rd Division Rear HQ	20 vehicles
8th Middlesex Regiment HQ	15 vehicles
Field Hygiene Section	15 vehicles
15 Field Dressing Station	10 vehicles
59th Anti-Tank Regiment Royal Artillery	84 vehicles
110th Light Anti-Aircraft Regiment RA	50 vehicles
Group 3 Royal Army Service Corps	250 vehicles
15th GHQ Troops Royal Engineers	187 vehicles

Total 1005 Vehicles

Appendix 2

After the 5th Duke of Cornwall's Light Infantry were over-run in their trenches at Pressagny l'Orgueilleux, during the early morning of 27 August, their commanding officer, Lieutenant-Colonel George Taylor decided to issue a 'Special Order of the Day' in order to stress the importance of holding the left flank of the bridgehead:

SPECIAL ORDER OF THE DAY

1. The task of this battalion is to hold the LEFT flank of the bridgehead. This is to enable armour to get across and push ahead with all speed. Therefore, this battalion WILL defend the LEFT flank, and by defend I mean TO THE LAST MAN and THE LAST ROUND.
2. In this close country the enemy may infiltrate behind you: but remember – if you hold your FIRE he can't locate you, and if he can't locate you, he'll walk straight into your trap; and if he walks into your trap, every bullet you fire will kill a German. Therefore; HOLD YOUR FIRE.
3. And finally this position WILL be held TO THE LAST MAN AND THE LAST ROUND.

G. Taylor – LT. COL.
Commander 5 D.C.L.I.

BLA
27 August 1944

Dist. Down to and incl. Sec. Comds.

Appendix 3

The main counter-attack against the Wessex Division's bridgehead was launched by Battle Group Schrader on 27 August. During that day, a copy of the order for the attack was captured:

OPERATIONAL ORDER FOR BATTLE GROUP SCHRADER

BN HQ 1020hrs.   27th August 1944

Order for attack by Battle Group Schrader
1) Patrol reports indicate that the enemy in the northern part of the Foret de Vernon is still weak. In the S.E. part the enemy are attempting to press us to the East.
2) Battle Group Schrader will attack at 1130 hours with,
    6/Gren Regt 149 right,
    1/Gren Regt 148,
    5/Gren Regt 148,
    and 4/Div Fus Bn 49.
    First objective track Château Madeleine-Foret de Tilly, thence S.E.
    1/Div Fus Bn 49 will first secure edge of wood west of Bois Jérôme – St Ouen and join in attack on my order.
    3/Gren Regt 149 remains at my disposal at Château Saulseuses.
3) The coys taking part in the attack, see para 2, will carry out the closest liaison.
4) I direct the greatest possible use to be made of own heavy weapons. We cannot allow that only the artillery support the infantry.
5) The attack will be supported along the main road leading to Vernon from the N.E. by three Tiger tanks.

(signed) SCHRADER

Distribution. As per. warning orders.

Appendix 4

The order for the attack by Battle Group Schrader was captured by the 43rd Division and was issued to all battalions the next day, together with comments on the order by the intelligence section:

COMMENTS ON BATTLE GROUP SCHRADER OPERATIONAL ORDER

1) First objective believed to be track 453753-476744.
2) This motley collection of coys had little time to carry out 'closest liaison', the attack being timed for 1130 hrs. and the order signal at 1020hrs. In fact the POW from 6/Gren Regt 149 stated his coy. was to have made a counter attack yesterday but the order arrived too late to be acted upon.
3) The three Tiger tanks have also been referred to by two POWS. One (from 5/Gren Regt 148) stated they were Wehrmacht and one was 'shot up'; another (from 4/Fus Bn 149) saw three which he believed were SS. He had heard there were twelve altogether.

   If the Wehrmacht theory was correct, they were probably belonging to 205 Heavy Tank Bn. which was previously reported in the area. If they are in fact SS, then they probably belong to 1 SS PANZER Division which is at present unlocated.
4) 149 Div Fus Bn has evidently been re-designated 49 Div Fus Bn.

Appendix 5

COMPOSITION OF THE 43RD WESSEX DIVISION:

129 Brigade:
    4th Somerset Light Infantry
    4th Wiltshires
    5th Wiltshires
130 Brigade:
    7th Hampshires
    4th Dorsets
    5th Dorsets
214 Brigade:
    7th Somerset Light Infantry
    1st Worcestershires
    5th Duke of Cornwall's Light Infantry

43rd Reconnaissance Regiment (5th Gloucestershire Regiment)
94th Field Regiment Royal Artillery
112th Field Regiment Royal Artillery
179th Field Regiment Royal Artillery
59th Anti-Tank Regiment Royal Artillery
110th Light Anti-Aircraft Regiment Royal Artillery
43rd Division Royal Engineers:
    260 Field Company Royal Engineers
    204 Field Company Royal Engineers
    553 Field Company Royal Engineers
    207 Field Park Company Royal Engineers
8th Middlesex Machine-Gun Battalion
43rd Division Royal Signals
Medical:
    129 Field Ambulance
    130 Field Ambulance
    214 Field Ambulance
    14 Field Dressing Station
    15 Field Dressing Station
    38 Field Hygiene Unit
    306 Mobile Laundry and Bath Unit

Royal Electrical and Mechanical Engineers:
　　129 Brigade Workshop REME
　　130 Brigade Workshop REME
　　214 Brigade Workshop REME
Royal Army Ordnance Corps:
　　43 Division Ordnance Field Park
Royal Army Service Corps:
　　504 Company RASC
　　505 Company RASC
　　506 Company RASC
　　54 Company RASC
57th Provost Company
54th Field Cash Office
Postal and Education Officers

Index